How to
Write Tests
for Students

The Authors

Patrick W. Miller is President of Patrick W. Miller and Associates, training and management consultants, Munster, Indiana. He is the author of *Nonverbal Communication*, and coauthor of *Teacher-Written Student Tests: A Guide for Planning, Creating, Administering, and Assessing*, published by NEA.

Harley E. Erickson is Professor Emeritus, Department of Educational Psychology and Foundations, University of Northern Iowa, Cedar Falls. He is coauthor of *Teacher-Written Student Tests: A Guide for Planning, Creating, Administering, and Assessing*.

How to
Write Tests
for Students

Patrick W. Miller
Harley E. Erickson

nea PROFESSIONAL LIBRARY

National Education Association
Washington, D.C.

Acknowledgments

We wish to thank our wives and children for their patience, understanding, and support during our work on this publication. We wish to express our appreciation to Stanley P. Lyle and O. R. Schmidt for reviewing the manuscript. And a special thank you to Joy and Tatum Miller for their help in inputting and proofreading copy. We also wish to express our appreciation to Bill Sinclair for his professional drawings.

— Patrick W. Miller
Harley E. Erickson

Parts of the material used in this publication have been adapted from *Teacher-Written Student Tests: A Guide for Planning, Creating, Administering, and Assessing*, by Patrick W. Miller and Harley E. Erickson.

Printing History
   First Printing: May 1990
   Second Printing: September 1992

Note

The opinions expressed in this publication should not be construed as representing the policy or position of the National Education Association. Materials published by the NEA Professional Library are intended to be discussion documents for teachers who are concerned with specialized interests of the profession.

Library of Congress Cataloging in Publication Data

Miller, Patrick W.
   How to write tests for students / Patrick W. Miller, Harley E. Erickson.
      p. cm—(NEA aspects of learning)
   ''Parts of the material used in this publication have been adapted from Teacher-written students tests''—T.p. verso.
   Includes bibliographical references.
   ISBN 0–8106–3008–7
   1. Examinations—Design and construction.   2. Examinations—Interpretation.   3. Grading and marking (Students)   I. Erickson. Harley E.   II. Miller, Patrick W.   Teacher-written student tests. III. National Education Association of the United States. IV. Title.   V. Series.
LB3060.65.M53   1990
371.2'61—dc20

90–31243
                                                                CIP

CONTENTS

INTRODUCTION

Testing is a part of the student learning process. The development of a good test containing true-false, multiple-choice, matching, and essay items is a difficult and time-consuming task. Many classroom teachers have received inadequate instruction in planning and developing tests that accurately measure student achievement.

How to Write Tests for Students offers guidelines, practical suggestions, and examples for constructing better tests. It is divided into six chapters: Planning Tests, Developing Tests, Assembling and Administering Tests, Interpreting Test Results, Assessing Test Items, and Improving Test Validity and Reliability. Each chapter concludes with review questions and activities, which apply the information presented. In addition, the publication contains four appendixes: a description of hierarchical levels for the affective, cognitive, and psychomotor domains; sample verbs for writing instructional objectives; a listing of selected computer software resources for test generation and analysis; and sample test items from various curriculum areas. Also included are a glossary of terms and a comprehensive bibliography.

The most effective way to use this book is to read it from beginning to end and to review the sample test items (Appendix D) for the appropriate curriculum area. Although *How to Write Tests for Students* is structured sequentially, some readers may choose to skim certain chapters and concentrate on others. In either case, the publication will be useful to all middle and secondary school teachers and administrators, as well as to those preparing to enter the teaching profession.

Chapter 1

PLANNING TESTS

Classroom teachers usually assess student achievement at the end of an instructional unit. Developing a test that accurately measures achievement requires careful planning. This planning includes an examination of student behaviors previously identified in the instructional objectives.

INSTRUCTIONAL OBJECTIVES

Classroom teachers are responsible for writing objectives that describe the behaviors expected of students. An *objective* is a communication device that specifies the knowledge, skills, and attitudes expected of students at the end of an instructional unit. Teachers should write and use objectives because they (1) identify expected outcomes for students, and provide information for administrators and parents as well; (2) form a basis for sequencing instructional content; and (3) establish a basis for evaluating student achievement. Some teachers write objectives with three components: (1) conditions, (2) performance, and (3) criteria. Others write objectives that explicitly state only the performance expected of students; they do not include a condition or criterion.

A *condition* identifies important resources or restrictions.

A *performance* specifies an observable behavior or competency.

A *criterion* specifies a standard for satisfactory performance.

EXAMPLE 1.1

Objective Format

Given (specify condition), the student will (insert performance statement) with performance satisfactory if (specify criterion).

Objective (containing condition, performance, and criterion)

Given a plant taxonomy, the student will **identify** at least *five of seven leaves* collected during a class field trip.

Key: condition   **performance**   *criterion*

EXAMPLE 1.2

Objective (with performance only)

The student will solve equations with one unknown.

Objectives are classified in the three learning domains: affective, cognitive, and psychomotor. Each domain has levels or subdivisions that require increasingly more complex student behaviors. Appendix A provides a complete description of the hierarchical levels for all three learning domains.

Affective objectives emphasize feelings, emotions, attitudes, and values. The major levels (from lowest to highest) are receiving, responding, valuing, organization, and characterization by a value complex.

EXAMPLE 1.3

Objective (affective domain)

The student will establish cooperative working relationships with peers.

Cognitive objectives emphasize intellectual tasks. The cognitive domain includes the largest proportion of educational objectives. These vary from simple recall of material to synthesizing and evaluating new ideas. The major levels (from lowest to highest) are knowledge, comprehension, application, analysis, synthesis, and evaluation.

EXAMPLE 1.4

Objective (cognitive domain)

The student will write an essay on the pros and cons of capital punishment.

Psychomotor objectives emphasize skill development and require neuromuscular coordination. Most objectives in this domain are used in physical education or trade and technical areas. The major levels (from lowest to highest) are perception, set, guided response, mechanism, complex overt response, adaptation, and origination.

EXAMPLE 1.5

Objective (psychomotor domain)

The student will weld ferrous and nonferrous metals.

Since most instructional objectives are in the cognitive domain, it is imperative that teachers understand the levels in this domain in order to develop appropriate test items.

Knowledge objectives require students to remember facts, principles, terms, customs, traditions, categories, rules, formulas, procedures, and criteria.

EXAMPLE 1.6

Objective (cognitive domain—knowledge level)

The student will match artists with paintings.

Comprehension objectives require students to describe, illustrate, summarize, interpret, or note consequences of ideas or methods.

EXAMPLE 1.7

Objective (cognitive domain—comprehension level)

The student will translate Spanish into English.

Application objectives require students to apply previously learned ideas, methods, or procedures in a setting that is different from the original learning experience.

EXAMPLE 1.8

Objective (cognitive domain—application level)

The student will calculate the perimeter of a nine-sided figure.

Analysis objectives require students to separate ideas into constituent parts in order to note relationships between the parts and the whole.

EXAMPLE 1.9

Objective (cognitive domain—analysis level)

The student will compare the responsibilities of the three branches of government of the United States.

Synthesis objectives require students to formulate new thoughts from previously learned material.

EXAMPLE 1.10

Objective (cognitive domain—synthesis level)

The student will develop a procedure for testing hypotheses.

Evaluation objectives require students to judge (assess) the value of ideas, methods, or procedures using appropriate criteria.

EXAMPLE 1.11

Objective (cognitive domain—evaluation level)

The student will critique two oral speeches presented in class.

Appendix B contains lists of sample verbs used to identify specific student behaviors and verbs used in various curriculum areas. These lists should be helpful to teachers when writing objectives that describe observable behaviors in the three learning domains.

TEST ITEMS

Test items should directly relate to specific behaviors identified in the instructional objectives. They should be written to reflect the specific domains and levels identified by the objectives. For example, if the objective required the students to synthesize, a test item that required only comprehension would be inappropriate. Synthesizing and comprehending do not require the same behavioral performance; consequently the objective and test item would not correspond. Test items should also assess the student's ability in a particular domain. For example, if the objective required the student to repair a ten-speed bicycle, a test item that required the student to list the repairs would be inappropriate. Repairing is a psychomotor activity, whereas listing is a cognitive activity at the lowest level.

All secondary curriculum areas place varying degrees of emphasis on instructional objectives in the three domains. Most teacher-written objectives, however, are usually classified in the three lowest levels of the cognitive domain. Attainment of objectives in these levels is appropriately assessed by true-false, multiple-choice, and matching test items. Objectives in the three highest levels of the cognitive domain are usually assessed by essay test items or more complex choice-type items.

Knowledge test items require recall or recognition of information in substantially the same form as the instruction. Rephrasing, inversion of sentences, and similar form changes do not remove a test item from this level.

Comprehension test items require interpretation of a principle in a manner that differs from the instruction, but that implies the principle.

Application test items require use of a previously learned principle in a new setting. These items differ from comprehension items in that they do not imply the required principle. Examples of such items are quantitative problems in mathematics and science.

Higher-level test items in the cognitive domain require analysis, synthesis, or evaluation of complex situations with appropriate generalizations or inferences.

EXAMPLE 1.12

Objective (cognitive domain—knowledge level)

The student will match chemical elements with abbreviations.

Matching Test Items

Match the chemical elements found in column I with the abbreviations from column II.

	I		II
C	1. Copper	A.	Ag
B	2. Gold	B.	Au
D	3. Mercury	C.	Cu
A	4. Silver	D.	Hg
G	5. Tin	E.	Me
		F.	Si
		G.	Sn

EXAMPLE 1.13

Objective (cognitive domain—comprehension level)

The student will identify the dominant "tone" of a poem.

Multiple-Choice Test Item

The tone of Cummings' poem *Among Crumbling People* is
   A. jaunty and bantering.
   B. sarcastic.
   C. silly.
  *D. sorrowful.

EXAMPLE 1.14

Objective (cognitive domain—application level)

The student will calculate the area of a circle given the circumference.

Multiple-Choice Test Item

If the circumference of a circle is 44 centimeters, the area in centimeters squared is
   A. 78
  *B. 154
   C. 308
   D. 1,078

EXAMPLE 1.15

Objective (cognitive domain—analysis level)

The student will compare and contrast research designs.

Essay Test Item

Compare and contrast experimental research, quasi-experimental research, and ex post facto research designs in terms of
   • methodology,
   • appropriate analysis techniques, and
   • interpretation and generalization of results.

The final step in test planning is to determine the appropriate number of test items to write for each level of the cognitive domain. This requires a careful analysis and classification of the instructional objectives. If, for example, the analysis reveals that 50 percent of the objectives are classified as knowledge, then 50 percent of the test items should assess recall of the facts and principles taught in the instructional unit. If the analysis indicates that the remaining objectives are classified as 25 percent comprehension, 15 percent application, and 10 percent higher levels, then appropriate test items should be written to reflect this instructional emphasis.

REVIEW QUESTIONS AND ACTIVITIES

Questions

1. What are the three components of an objective?

2. What are the subdivisions of the cognitive domain?

3. What are the subdivisions of the affective domain?

4. What are the subdivisions of the psychomotor domain?

5. What domain includes the largest proportion of educational objectives?

6. What kind of test items (e.g., true-false, multiple-choice, matching, essay) are used to assess the highest levels of cognitive learning?

7. What determines the appropriate number of items for a test in the cognitive domain?

Activities

1. Underline and label the condition, performance, and criterion of the following student objective:

   In a field setting, students will weld 15″ pipe that will withstand a 3,000 psi pressure test.

2. Match each type of learning in column I with the most appropriate domain in column II.

I	II
____ 1. Comprehending ideas	A. Affective
____ 2. Applying principles	B. Cognitive
____ 3. Carving wood	C. Psychomotor
____ 4. Valuing quality work	
____ 5. Evaluating concepts	

3. Write an objective that focuses on students becoming punctual workers.

4. Write an objective that requires a student to accomplish a high-level psychomotor task.

5. Develop a multiple-choice test item to measure an application-level cognitive concept.

6. Develop an essay test item to measure a high-level cognitive concept.

Chapter 2

DEVELOPING TESTS

The most frequently used teacher-made tests to assess student achievement are true-false, multiple-choice, matching, and essay. Each of these tests has distinct advantages and disadvantages. True-false, multiple-choice, and matching tests are relatively easy to write; they sample a large amount of content, and are quickly and objectively scored. These tests are frequently limited to facts, they encourage guessing, and they usually do not measure higher levels of cognitive learning (analysis, synthesis, and evaluation). The major advantage of the essay test is that it requires students to demonstrate attainment of instructional objectives in the higher levels of the cognitive domain. In addition, the essay test allows students to express themselves in their own words. Its major disadvantage is the subjectivity associated with rating student responses.

Several general and specific guidelines will help teachers when they write any type of classroom test.

GENERAL GUIDELINES

The general guidelines for developing classroom tests include the following:

- Test items should be directly related to the instructional objectives.
- Test items should be clear and free of ambiguities.
- Test items should use vocabulary appropriate to the educational level of the students.
- Test items should be grammatically correct and free from spelling and typing errors.
- Test items should be realistic and practical; that is, they should call for information that students must use.
- One test item should not be based on the response to another, nor should it provide a clue to other items.
- Test items should minimize or avoid the use of textbook or stereotyped language.
- Test items should cite authorities for statements that might be considered debatable or based on opinion.
- Test items should avoid complex sentences.
- Test items should use the simplest method for recording responses.
- Test directions should be clear and complete.

SPECIFIC GUIDELINES

In addition to general guidelines, specific guidelines should be used in developing true-false, multiple-choice, matching, and essay test items. These guidelines, coupled with examples, are designed to provide teachers with a sense of direction for constructing appropriate test items.

True-False Items

The true-false test consists of statements that are either true or false. The student must read the statements and choose one of two alternatives: true or false, yes or no, right or wrong, or plus or minus (+ or −). The following are guidelines for constructing true-false test items:

- Each test item should focus on a single important idea.
- A test item should be false because it contains an important concept that is incorrect, not because it contains an insignificant error.
- Each test item should be written as an affirmative rather than a negative statement.

EXAMPLE 2.1

Poor   T   F   James Madison was not a President of the United States.

Good   T   F   James Madison was a President of the United States.

- Test items should never use double negatives.

EXAMPLE 2.2

Poor   T   F   Watergate was not an instance of unauthorized entry.

Good   T   F   Watergate was an instance of unauthorized entry.

- Test items should be brief, but not at the expense of clarity. Avoid sentences in excess of 20 words because they are guessed true more often than false. A lengthy statement containing dependent clauses and phrases reduces the probability that an item is false.
- Test items containing specific citations or enumerations should be used with caution. Such statements are more likely to be true than false.
- Test items should not use specific determiners, such as *all*, *always*, *exactly*, *never*, *totally*, *entirely*, *completely*, *solely*, *fully*, *absolutely*, *exclusively*, *only*, *none*, *nothing*, and *alone*, because they are likely to be false.
- Test items should be true or false without qualification. Statements containing qualifiers, such as *sometimes*, *maybe*, *often*, *several*, *as a rule*, *should*, *may*, *most*, *some*, and *generally*, are more likely to be true than false.
- Test items that are true should not be consistently longer than those that are false.
- Tests should consist of approximately equal numbers of true and false statements.

EXAMPLE 2.3

Sample True-False Items

  __F__   1. $X = 8$ in the equation $3X + 6 = 18$.

  __T__   2. The area of a rectangle 5 cm wide × 8 cm long is 40 cm².

15

Multiple-Choice Items

Each item in a multiple-choice test consists of a stem and alternatives (a correct response and several distractors). The stem presents a statement or question; the correct response provides a solution or answer. The distractors are incorrect choices that should attract students who have not mastered the material, yet should not confuse students who have attained mastery.

There are several guidelines for writing stems and alternatives.

Guidelines for Developing Stems

The guidelines for developing stems of multiple-choice items include the following:

- Stems should be stated as briefly and concisely as possible.
- Stems should be concerned with only one central problem.
- Stems should be direct questions or incomplete statements.
- Stems should be stated positively.
- Stems should include as much of the item as possible so that students need not reread the same material in each alternative.

EXAMPLE 2.4

Poor   If a gas is compressed
       *A. its temperature increases.
       B. its temperature decreases.
       C. its temperature remains the same.
       D. its temperature sometimes increases and sometimes decreases.

Good   Compressing a gas causes its temperature to
       *A. increase.
       B. decrease.
       C. remain the same.
       D. fluctuate between increase and decrease.

- Stems should not use "a" or "an" as the final word if it serves as a clue to the correct response.

EXAMPLE 2.5

Poor   Oak is a material that is an
       *A. open-grain wood.
       B. closed-grain wood.
       C. soft wood.
       D. hardboard.

Good   Oak is a material that is a/an
       *A. open-grain wood.
       B. closed-grain wood.
       C. soft wood.
       D. hardboard.

Guidelines for Developing Alternatives

Multiple-choice item alternatives consist of three or four distractors (incorrect choices) and the correct response. The guidelines for developing these alternatives include the following:

- Alternatives must include one choice that is clearly the best (correct) response; the remaining alternatives should appear plausible to the uninformed or partially informed student. An alternative should not be included solely for the purpose of humor.
- Alternatives should be grammatically correct and consistent with the stem.
- Alternatives should include the statements "none of the above" or "all of the above" with caution.
- Alternatives should use the appropriate punctuation marks.
- Alternatives for each test item should be approximately equal in length.
- Alternatives should be arranged so that the correct responses for all multiple-choice items occur in a random order.
- Alternatives should be as brief as possible.
- The format of the test should be consistent.

EXAMPLE 2.6

Sample Multiple-Choice Items

1. The measure of central tendency computed when it is desired to avoid the effect of extremely high or low scores is the
   A. mean.
   *B. median.
   C. mode.
   D. variance.

2. The probability of observing two heads and one tail in a single toss of three coins is
   A. 1/8.
   B. 2/8.
   *C. 3/8.
   D. 5/8.

Matching Items

There are times when matching test items are most appropriate for assessing student achievement in an instructional unit. Matching tests require students to respond by pairing statements or words in two columns of related material. The typical matching exercise consists of a list of statements in column I (primary column) and a list of responses in column II (response column).

Specific guidelines for developing matching test items include the following:

- Directions should clearly describe the contents of columns I and II and the basis for matching.
- Matching exercises should consist of homogeneous material (for example, historical events and dates).
- The entire matching exercise should be on the same page.
- Responses in column II should be arranged in some systematic manner: alphabetically, chronologically, or, in the case of numerical responses, in ascending or descending order.

- Column II should contain only one correct match for each statement in column I.
- In most cases, column II should contain more responses than needed for matching with the statements in column I.
- The statements in column I should normally be longer than the responses in column II because the statements should serve as stems and the responses as alternatives. This provides a more efficient visual arrangement for students.

EXAMPLE 2.7

Sample Matching Items

Directions: Match the inventions found in column I with the inventors in column II.

	I		II
C	1. Atlantic cable	A.	Colt
I	2. cotton gin	B.	Edison
F	3. electric starter	C.	Field
E	4. sewing machine	D.	Franklin
H	5. steam engine	E.	Howe
G	6. wireless telegraphy	F.	Kettering
		G.	Marconi
		H.	Watt
		I.	Whitney

Essay Items

Essay test items usually consist of questions that require the student to demonstrate attainment of instructional objectives in the higher levels of the cognitive domain. Responses should indicate the student's ability to organize facts and ideas in a clear and meaningful way.

A helpful resource for teachers preparing essay test items is *Teaching Writing in the Content Areas: Senior High School* (by Stephen N. Tchudi and Joanne Yates [National Education Association, 1983]). Emphasizing the relationship between written expression and understanding of content, these authors recommend designing essay examinations that make it easier for students to produce good writing, as well as to "display their content knowledge as fully and clearly as they are able." To accomplish this, they suggest giving students several options—a dialogue, a story, an on-the-scene report, an interview, a scenario—rather than confining them to an essay to answer such examination questions. According to Tchudi and Yates, most content knowledge is expressed clearly and fully in different ways.

To help students organize their facts and ideas, especially when time is limited, teachers can remind students to apply what they know about the writing process to the examination. For example, they should divide their available time into three parts: "a brief time for prewriting (thinking and planning), a longer time for writing, and a short time for revision and copyediting." Tchudi and Yates also offer specific strategies for each part of the writing process.

Guidelines for developing essay questions include the following:

- Indicate a limit (space, words, time) for each item.
- State items clearly and identify specifically what the student is to accomplish.
- Develop a sample answer (before administering the test) that indicates the main points expected in the response.

18

EXAMPLE 2.8

Sample Essay Item

During this class period, write an essay that explains your position on the issue of capital punishment. Consider both sides of the issue and provide pro and con arguments you consider relevant.

Points for Grading

Pro Arguments:
- Society must protect itself against violent criminals.   5
- Society must establish deterrents to crime.   5
- Death is a just punishment.   5

Con Arguments:
- Death penalties are unjust.   5
- Execution is not a morally defensible response to crime.   5
- Capital punishment does not deter crime.   5

- Two individual counters and/or critiques to relevant pro/con arguments.   10
- Individual's position.   10

Total   50

REVIEW QUESTIONS AND ACTIVITIES

Questions

1. What are the advantages and disadvantages of true-false, multiple-choice, and matching test items?

2. What are the advantages and disadvantages of essay test items?

3. What are specific guidelines for writing true-false test items?

4. What are specific guidelines for writing multiple-choice test items?

5. What are specific guidelines for writing matching test items?

6. What are specific guidelines for writing essay test items?

Activities

1. Write a true-false test item

2. Write a multiple-choice test item.

3. Write matching test items.

4. Write an essay test item.

Chapter 3

ASSEMBLING AND ADMINISTERING TESTS

After carefully preparing test items, it is important that teachers give similar attention to assembling the items, preparing test directions, and administering the test. Inattention to these factors may adversely affect the test results.

ASSEMBLING TEST ITEMS

To create better tests, teachers should (1) review instructional objectives, (2) select or write items that assess these objectives, and (3) properly arrange the items in a final test form.

To improve existing tests, teachers should review the items, rewriting those that (1) are unclear, (2) have poor (implausible) distractors, (3) are too easy, (4) are too difficult, and (5) have technical and/or grammatical errors. One way to go about this process is to ask a colleague to review the test and supply information about individual items as well as the test as a whole. This "teacher review method" can provide information about item ambiguity and other flaws that may have gone unnoticed.

There are several guidelines to follow when assembling test items:

- Arrange items by type (all matching together, etc.). This technique provides a consistent response mode for students. Directions should precede different item types.
- Arrange items according to instructional content. This technique allows students to see relationships among test items. It also provides the teacher an opportunity to compare test content with instructional objectives.
- Arrange items in order of increasing difficulty. This arrangement may help relieve test anxiety and enable students to proceed in a timely manner to later items. No easy test items should be unanswered because of time limitations.

PREPARING TEST DIRECTIONS

A good test includes directions that explain how to respond to the item(s). Poorly written directions can mislead and confuse students. Directions should state clearly and concisely what, how, where, and when students should answer. Some tests (e.g., true-false and multiple-choice) require simple directions; others (e.g., matching and essay) may require more complex directions.

The guidelines for developing test directions include the following:

- Use a clear, succinct writing style.
- Create directions that stand out by using different type style or size, underlining type, or using bold type.
- Check directions for misunderstandings or inconsistencies.
- Have colleagues read for clarity and understanding.
- Use a parallel format for all test item sections.
- Provide a sample test item with the directions.

EXAMPLE 3.1

DIRECTIONS: *Circle the letter for the best answer to each question.*

Sample How many days are in a week?
A. 3
B. 5
C. 6
(D.) 7

1. How many centimeters are in one meter?

A. 10
B. 12
C. 100
D. 1000

2. How many millimeters are in one meter?

A. 10
B. 12
C. 100
D. 1000

Sample directions for use with true-false, multiple-choice, and matching test items for both answer sheet and test booklet responses follow.

True-False Directions

Answer Sheet: The following statements are either true or false. If you believe the statement is true, darken the first space on the answer sheet that corresponds to the item number with a #2 pencil. If you believe the statement is false, darken the second space on the answer sheet that corresponds to the item number.

EXAMPLE 3.2

1. Copper is a conductor of heat and electricity.

Answer Sheet

	T	F			
1.	A	B	C	D	E
	▅▅	═══	═══	═══	═══

Test Booklet: The following statements are true or false. If you believe the statement is true, write T in the blank preceding the item number. If you believe the statement is false, write F in the blank preceding the item number.

EXAMPLE 3.3

 T 1. Copper is a conductor of heat and electricity.

Multiple-Choice Directions

Answer Sheet: The following items include a statement or question with four alternatives, only one of which is correct. Indicate your selection of the alternative that correctly completes the item or answers the question by darkening the space below the corresponding letter on the answer sheet with a #2 pencil.

EXAMPLE 3.4

  2. The ability to do work or perform some action is
      A. energy.
      B. kilowatts.
      C. power.
      D. wave motion.

Answer Sheet

2.   A   B   C   D   E

Test Booklet: The following items include a statement or question with four alternatives, only one of which is correct. Indicate your selection of the alternative that correctly completes the item or answers the question by placing the corresponding letter in the blank to the left of the item number.

EXAMPLE 3.5

  <u>A</u> 2. The ability to do work or perform some action is
      A. energy.
      B. kilowatts.
      C. power.
      D. wave motion.

Matching Directions

Answer Sheet: The following matching items (in Example 3.6) have two columns. Column 1 describes four measurement instruments. Column II lists five tests or inventories. Match each description in column I with the test or inventory in column II by darkening the space below the corresponding letter on the answer sheet with a #2 pencil.

Test Booklet: The following matching items (in Example 3.7) have two columns. Column I describes four measurement instruments. Column II lists five tests or inventories. Match each description in column I with the test or inventory in column II by placing the appropriate letter in the blank to the left of the item number.

23

EXAMPLE 3.6

I	II
3. Provides a measure of personal likes and dislikes.	A. Achievement test
4. Measures potential ability or capacity to learn various skills and acquire new knowledge.	B. Aptitude test
5. Measures amount of knowledge or skills child has acquired in particular subject field.	C. Attitude measure
6. Measures global capacity to act purposefully, think logically, and deal with environment.	D. General mental ability test
	E. Interest inventory

Answer Sheet

	A	B	C	D	E
3.	===	===	■■■	===	===
4.	===	■■■	===	===	===
5.	■■■	===	===	===	===
6.	===	===	===	■■■	===

EXAMPLE 3.7

I	II
C 3. Provides a measure of personal likes and dislikes.	A. Achievement test
B 4. Measures potential ability or capacity to learn various skills and acquire new knowledge.	B. Aptitude test
A 5. Measures amount of knowledge or skills child has acquired in particular subject field.	C. Attitude measure
D 6. Measures global capacity to act purposefully, think logically, and deal with environment.	D. General mental ability test
	E. Interest inventory

ADMINISTERING TESTS

When administering tests, teachers must provide all students with the opportunity to demonstrate attainment of the instructional objectives. Therefore, a careful consideration of the physical setting and the psychological factors that may affect students' test results is important.

Physical Setting

Since most tests are administered in classrooms, it is important that teachers attempt to provide an atmosphere conducive to successful test taking. Ideal testing conditions include the following:

- Ample student space
- Proper lighting and ventilation
- Comfortable temperature and reasonable air circulation.

Some classroom conditions are beyond the teacher's control; others, however, can be modified by a sensitive teacher. For example, if the afternoon sun is creating a glare for certain students, adjusting the window covering could eliminate the problem. In other words, teacher sensitivity to students' reactions can improve the physical setting.

Attentiveness to distractions from hallways, adjacent rooms, or outside the building is also important. Although teachers cannot anticipate many of these distractions, they can avoid most of them by carefully selecting the best time to administer the test.

Psychological Conditions

The psychological atmosphere associated with testing is often overlooked even though these factors can affect test results as much as, if not more than, the physical conditions. If students feel tense, overanxious, or pressured, their performance during testing may be hindered. Teachers should be especially alert to these factors so that testing situations may facilitate accurate assessment.

Teachers can create a positive testing atmosphere by explaining the reason for the test and adequately preparing students. They can best accomplish this by reviewing the instructional content to be covered by the test and providing students with sample test items. The nature of the test and the amount of time students need for preparation will dictate the best time for this orientation. It may be a week or more before the test, or it may be immediately before the test. Keep in mind, however, that, even with careful preparation, some students will still be apprehensive because of the evaluative nature of testing.

REVIEW QUESTIONS AND ACTIVITIES

Questions

1. What are the guidelines for assembling test items?

2. Why is it important to write clear test directions?

3. What physical setting conditions must be considered before administering a test?

4. What psychological conditions must be considered before administering a test?

Activities

1. Write a set of directions for true-false, multiple-choice, matching, and essay test items.

2. Describe how the teacher should prepare a classroom before administering a test.

Chapter 4

INTERPRETING TEST RESULTS

All teachers are involved in scoring tests and interpreting results. Objectively scored tests (true-false, multiple-choice, matching) use items with only one correct answer; they should yield the same results no matter who scores the test. Subjectively scored tests (short-answer, essay) use items with several possible answers; different results often occur when two or more individuals score these tests.

Test results should be provided to students as feedback as soon as possible after the testing situation. To interpret test results, teachers can use raw scores, frequency distributions, ranks, percentile ranks, measures of central tendency, measures of dispersion, and z-scores and T-scores.

RAW SCORES

A *raw score* is the actual score a student receives on a test. Raw scores are usually easy to obtain and provide quick feedback; however, they are difficult to interpret and can be misleading. For example, a raw score of 64 on an English test, if considered in relation to a traditional grading scale (90–100 = A, 80–89 = B, 70–79 = C, 60–69 = D, and 59 and below = F) and without additional information, would be interpreted as a D grade. If, on the other hand, the highest possible score on the test was 66, a raw score of 64 would represent 97% or an A grade.

FREQUENCY DISTRIBUTION

A *frequency distribution* is a tally of scores for a particular test arranged from highest to lowest. This display offers a degree of comparability by indicating how well one student did in relation to other students who completed the same test. Teachers use frequency distribution to present interpretative information to parents and administrators.

RANKS

Ranks indicate the position of a score in relation to other scores. They are used to clarify the meaning of a raw score on a test. Scores are assigned successive ranks from 1 to N beginning with the highest score. If two or more students received the same score on a test, the rank assigned to each student is determined by dividing the sum of the tied ranks by the number of students who received the score. For example, if two students received the highest score of 98 on a test, both students would be ranked 1.5 (ranks 1 + 2 divided by 2 students = 1.5 rank for both). If three students received the highest score of 98 on a test, all three students would receive a ranking of 2 (ranks 1 + 2 + 3 divided by 3 students = 2 rank for all three).

EXAMPLE 4.1

Frequency Distribution

Test Scores	Frequency	Rank	
95	1	1	
94	1	2	
91	1	3	
90	1	4	
89	1	5	
86	3	7	(6 + 7 + 8 divided by 3)
75	2	9.5	(9 + 10 divided by 2)
73	1	11	
72	1	12	

PERCENTILE RANKS

A *percentile rank* indicates the percentage of students in a class who obtained raw scores below a given score. For example, a percentile rank of 90 for a raw score of 85 indicates that 90 percent of the students in the group tested had raw scores lower than 85, and 10 percent had raw scores higher than 85. A percentile rank can be calculated using the frequency or rank of the score in the distribution.

FORMULA

Percentile Rank (using frequency)

$$PR = \frac{\text{number of test scores below score} + \frac{1}{2} \text{ at score}}{N \text{ (\# of students who completed test)}} \times 100$$

Percentile Rank (using rank)

$$PR = \frac{N \text{ (\# of students who completed test)} + .5 - \text{rank}}{N \text{ (\# of students who completed test)}} \times 100$$

MEASURES OF CENTRAL TENDENCY

Measures of central tendency include the mean, median, and mode. The *mean* is the arithmetic average of test scores. It is calculated by adding all the test scores in a distribution and dividing the sum of these scores by the number of students who took the test. The *median* is the middle test score in a list of scores from highest to lowest. It is the exact point in a distribution of ranked scores at which one-half or 50 percent of the scores fall above and below. The *mode* is the most frequent score (the score made by the largest number of students) in a frequency distribution. In a bimodal distribution two scores tie for most frequent occurrence. In a trimodal distribution three scores tie for most frequent occurrence. Distributions should be considered bimodal or trimodal only if the frequency of the tied scores is more than two.

EXAMPLE 4.2

Calculate the percentile rank for test score 75.

Test Scores	Frequency	Rank
95	1	1
94	1	2
91	1	3
90	1	4
89	1	5
86	3	7
75	2	9.5
73	1	11
72	1	12

$$PR \text{ (frequency)} = \frac{\text{number of test scores below 75} + \frac{1}{2} \text{ at 75}}{N} \times 100$$

$$PR = \frac{2 + 1}{12} \times 100 \qquad\qquad PR = \frac{3}{12} \times 100 = 25$$

$$PR \text{ (rank)} = \frac{N + .5 - \text{rank}}{N} \times 100$$

$$PR = \frac{12 + .5 - 9.5}{12} \times 100 \qquad\qquad PR = \frac{3}{12} \times 100 = 25$$

FORMULA

Mean

$$\text{Mean} = \overline{X} = \frac{\Sigma X}{N}$$

$\overline{X}$ = Mean
ΣX = Sum of test scores
N = Number of students who took the test

Normal Distribution

Bimodal Distribution

Trimodal Distribution

EXAMPLE 4.3

Calculate the mean for the following test scores:

Test Scores
X

81
80
79
75
72
71
70
69
67
66

$\Sigma X = 730$

$$\text{Mean} = \overline{X} = \frac{\Sigma X}{N} = \frac{730}{10} = 73.0$$

EXAMPLE 4.4

Calculate the median and mode for the following test score distribution:

Test Scores	Frequency	Tally
96	1	I
94	3	III
91	5	IIII
90	5	IIII
87	6	IIII I
85	8	IIII III
82	5	IIII
79	2	II
77	2	II
76	2	II
74	1	I

Median = Middle point in a distribution of test scores

Median = Middle point in a distribution of 40 test scores

Median = <u>86</u> (middle point between test scores 85 and 87)

Mode = Test score made by the largest number of students

Mode = <u>85</u> (test score made by 8 students)

MEASURES OF DISPERSION

The most common measures of dispersion used by teachers are the range and the standard deviation. The *range* is the difference between the highest and lowest scores on a test. For example, if the highest score on a test is 90 and the lowest score on the same test is 49, the range is 41 (90 − 49 = 41).

The range is used with measures of central tendency to describe the distribution of scores. If the distributions of test scores for two classes have different ranges, the test performance of the class with the larger range is more variable (more widely spread out along the score scale) than the class with the smaller range. For example, consider two groups of students who completed a 100-point test. The mean score for each class is 75; however, one class had test scores from 55 to 95 or a range of 40, and the second class had test scores from 65 to 85 or a range of 20. The test performance of the first class is more variable than that of the second class.

Standard deviation is a measure of dispersion that indicates how scores within a distribution deviate from the mean. In a normal distribution (bell-shaped curve), 68 percent of test scores lie between one standard deviation above the mean (34%) and one standard deviation below the mean (34%). Ninety-six percent (96%) of test scores lie between two standard deviations above the mean (48%) and two standard deviations below the mean (48%). Approximately 2 percent of the scores lie between two and three standard deviations above the mean and 2 percent of scores lie between two and three standard deviations below the mean.

Numerous human characteristics follow a normal distribution. For example, adult intelligence (Wechsler Adult Intelligence Scale) is distributed normally with a mean intelligence quotient (IQ) of 100 and a standard deviation of 15. Approximately 68 percent of people have IQs between 85 and 115 (between one standard deviation above and below the mean). Approximately 14 percent of individuals have IQs between 115 and 130 (between one and two standard deviations above the mean), and approximately 14 percent have IQs between 70 and 85 (between one and two standard deviations below the mean). An additional 2 percent of individuals have IQs between 130 and 145 (between two and three standard deviations above the mean) and 2 percent have IQs between 55 and 70 (between two and three standard deviations below the mean).

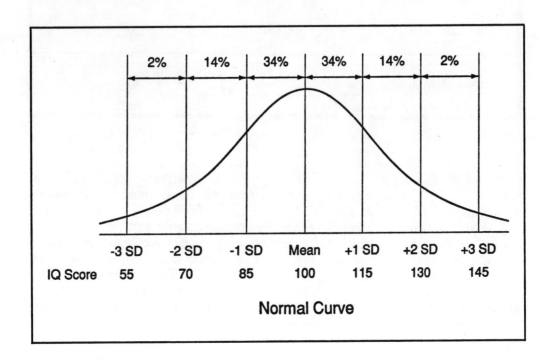

Normal Curve

$$\text{Standard Deviation} = \text{SD} = \sqrt{\frac{\Sigma x^2}{N}}$$

SD $\;=\;$ Standard Deviation
$\Sigma x^2 \;=\;$ Sum of squared differences the test scores are from the mean
N $\quad=\;$ Number of students who completed the test

EXAMPLE 4.5

Compute the mean and standard deviation for the following test scores:

Test Scores

X	x	x^2
45	5	25
44	4	16
42	2	4
41	1	1
39	−1	1
38	−2	4
38	−2	4
37	−3	9
36	−4	16
$\Sigma X = 360$		$\Sigma x^2 = 80$

$$\text{Mean} = \overline{X} = \frac{\Sigma X}{N} = \frac{360}{9} = 40.0$$

$$\text{Standard deviation} = \text{SD} = \sqrt{\frac{\Sigma x^2}{N}} = \sqrt{\frac{80}{9}} = \sqrt{8.89} = 2.98$$

A normal curve represents a normal or symmetrical distribution of scores. Distributions may also be skewed. A *skewed distribution* is an asymmetrical distribution with a majority of scores at one end. In a *negatively skewed* distribution the longer tail of the distribution extends toward the negative (left) end. In a *positively skewed* distribution the longer tail extends toward the positive (right) end. Skewness is determined by comparing the mean and median of a distribution of scores. When the mean and median are equal, the distribution displays symmetry. When the median and mean are not equal, the distribution is positively or negatively skewed. If class size is more than 25, most score distributions are negatively skewed for well-constructed and valid classroom unit tests.

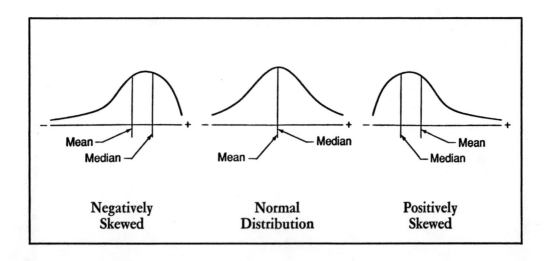

| Negatively Skewed | Normal Distribution | Positively Skewed |

Z-SCORES AND T-SCORES

A *z-score* represents the number of standard deviations of a raw score from the mean in a distribution. The mean and deviation must be calculated before the z-score is computed. All z-score distributions have a mean of zero and a standard deviation of one. Thus, a student with a z-score of +1.5 is 1½ standard deviations above the mean. Conversely, a student with a z-score of −1.5 is 1½ standard deviations below the mean.

A *T-score* also represents the number of standard deviations of a raw score from the mean. Unlike z-scores, T-scores do not use decimals or negative numbers. They have a mean of 50 and a standard deviation of 10. Thus, a student with a T-score of 65 is 1½ standard deviations above the mean. Conversely, a student with a T-score of 35 is 1½ standard deviations below the mean. To convert a z-score to a T-score, multiply the z-score by 10 and add 50. For example, a z-score of +2.0 is the same as a T-score of 70 ($2.0 \times 10 = 20 + 50 = 70$). Negative z-scores can also be converted to T-scores. For example, a z-score of −2.0 is the same as a T-score of 30 ($-2.0 \times 10 = -20 + 50 = 30$).

EXAMPLE 4.6

Calculate the z-score and T-score for test score 67.

Test Scores

X	x	x^2
81	8	64
80	7	49
79	6	36
75	2	4
72	−1	1
71	−2	4
70	−3	9
69	−4	16
67	−6	36
66	−7	49
$\Sigma X = 730$		$\Sigma x^2 = 268$

$$\text{Mean} = \overline{X} = \frac{\Sigma X}{N} = \frac{730}{10} = 73.0$$

$$\text{Standard deviation} = SD = \sqrt{\frac{\Sigma x^2}{N}} = \sqrt{\frac{268}{10}} = \sqrt{26.8} = 5.18$$

$$\text{z-score} = \frac{\text{Raw score} - \text{Mean}}{\text{Standard Deviation}} = \frac{67 - 73.0}{5.18} = \frac{-6.0}{5.18} = -1.16$$

$$\text{T-score} = 10\,(\text{z-score}) + 50 = 10\,(-1.16) + 50 = 38$$

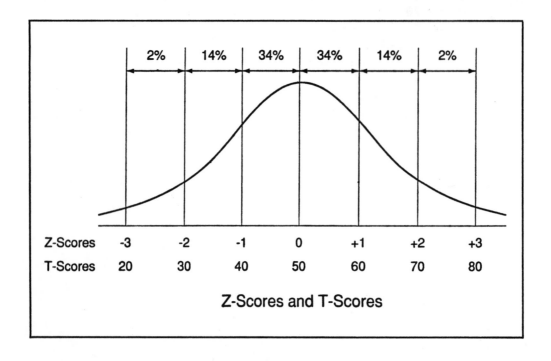

	2%	14%	34%	34%	14%	2%	
Z-Scores	-3	-2	-1	0	+1	+2	+3
T-Scores	20	30	40	50	60	70	80

Z-Scores and T-Scores

REVIEW QUESTIONS AND ACTIVITIES

Questions

1. What is a raw score?

2. What is a frequency distribution?

3. What is a percentile rank?

4. What is the mean?

5. What is the median?

6. What is the mode?

7. What is standard deviation?

8. What is the difference between a normal and a skewed distribution of scores?

9. What is the difference between a normal and a bimodal distribution of scores?

10. What are z-scores and T-scores?

Activities

1. Describe the advantages of reporting student performance using raw scores, ranks, and frequency distribution.

2. Calculate the mean for the following test scores:

Test Scores	Frequency
100	2
93	3
92	5
87	3
86	8
81	3
77	3
73	2
70	5
67	2
66	1
63	1

3. Calculate the median, mode, and range for the following test scores:

Test Scores	Frequency
96	1
94	3
91	5
90	5
87	6
85	8
82	5
79	2
77	2
76	2
74	1

4. Calculate the mean and standard deviation for the following test scores:

Test Scores	Frequency
95	1
94	1
91	1
90	1
89	1
86	3
75	1
73	1
72	1

5. Calculate the z-score and the T-score for test scores 73 and 95.

Test Scores	Frequency
95	1
94	1
91	1
90	1
89	1
86	3
75	1
73	1
72	1

6. Determine the rank and percentile rank for each of the following test scores:

Test Scores	Frequency
85	1
84	1
80	2
75	5
70	2
65	2
60	1

7. The following are raw scores from a test administered to a class of 20 students. Organize these scores into a frequency distribution and compute the
   a. mean, median, and mode;
   b. range and standard deviation; and
   c. z-score and T-score for each test score.

Test Scores

98	81	92	87	86
86	91	71	86	75
63	72	52	86	87
77	59	91	97	82

8. The following are raw scores from a test administered to a class of 30 students. Organize these scores into a frequency distribution and compute the
   a. mean, median, and mode;
   b. range and standard deviation; and
   c. z-score and T-score for each test score.

Test Scores

33	20	28	25	21
27	14	15	36	07
24	34	25	07	17
28	21	17	21	26
40	37	09	26	22
29	17	10	42	12

Chapter 5

ASSESSING TEST ITEMS

After scoring and returning a test, most teachers allow time for students to ask questions about specific items. This procedure provides the teacher with feedback about the entire test (directions, items, and scoring procedures), and it can also identify items that are ambiguous or otherwise flawed. Unfortunately, this informal feedback is often the only analysis teachers make before administering the test again. The entire test is more systematically appraised by using three techniques: analyzing an item response profile, calculating item difficulty, and determining item discrimination.

RESPONSE PROFILE

Determining the appropriateness or effectiveness of each test item requires an analysis of student responses. A *response profile* provides an index of the frequency of student responses to test alternatives. It is particularly valuable in identifying how well distractors work in multiple-choice items.

Suppose a class recently completed a test and, in addition to student feedback, the teacher desires more detailed information about each item. Examples 5.1 through 5.3 provide sample test items and response profiles for a class of 25 students. These examples illustrate the use of a response profile to determine how well each alternative functions in a multiple-choice item.

EXAMPLE 5.1

Test Item

If the odds in favor of an event occurring are 6 to 1, the probability of this event occurring is

    A. 1/7
    B. 1/6
  *C. 6/7
    D. 1/13

Response Profile

A	B	*C	D	(Alternatives)
4	6	15	0	(# of student responses)

The response profile for the item in Example 5.1 shows that no students responded to alternative D. This should immediately indicate to the teacher that alternative D needs revision if it is to be retained.

EXAMPLE 5.2

Test Item

On a true-false test of N items, the test score (A) is computed as the number right (R) minus the number wrong (W). If Joe responds to all the items and R are right, what score is recorded for Joe? (A, N, R)

$$*A. \quad A = 2R - N$$
$$B. \quad A = R - (R - N)$$
$$C. \quad A = R/N$$
$$D. \quad A = R - N$$

Response Profile

*A	B	C	D	(Alternatives)
8	5	6	6	(# of student responses)

The response profile for the item in Example 5.2 indicates that the item is faulty since almost equal numbers of students responded to the correct answer and the three distractors. This item should be examined for complexity as well as for appropriate relationship to the instructional objective(s).

EXAMPLE 5.3

Test Item

If you are involved in an automobile accident and an injury occurs, the first place you should call is the

    A. automobile repair center.
    *B. hospital.
    C. insurance company office.
    D. police station.

Response Profile

A	*B	C	D	(Alternatives)
2	8	3	12	(# of student responses)

Distractor D in example 5.3 should be carefully examined, since more students responded to it than to the keyed (*) alternative.

ITEM DIFFICULTY

Item difficulty indicates the proportion of students who responded correctly to a test item. The difficulty of an item is expressed on a scale from 0.00 to 1.00. A value of 0.00 indicates that no students responded correctly; a value of 1.00 indicates that all students responded correctly. For example, a difficulty index of .70 indicates that 70 percent of the students responded correctly to a particular item. Most test developers recommend a .30 to .70 difficulty range with an average item difficulty of .50. Test items with difficulty indexes above .70 are easy and those with difficulty indexes below .30 are difficult.

Item difficulty is calculated by the following formula:

FORMULA

$$\text{Item difficulty} = \frac{\text{\# of students responding correctly to test item}}{\text{\# of students responding to test item}}$$

Examples 5.4 and 5.5 provide sample test items with a response profile and an item difficulty calculation for a class of 25 students.

EXAMPLE 5.4

Test Item

The design principle that stresses the quality of equilibrium is

    *A. balance.
     B. proportion.
     C. unity.
     D. variety.

Response Profile

*A	B	C	D	(Alternatives)
18	3	2	2	(# of student responses)

Item Difficulty

$$\text{Item difficulty} = \frac{18}{25} = .72$$

Example 5.4 identifies a relatively easy item, since 72 percent of the students responded correctly. An item difficulty of .72 indicates that approximately three-fourths of the class demonstrated attainment of the instructional objective assessed by the item.

```
┌─────────────────────────────────────────────────────────────┐
│  EXAMPLE 5.5                                                  │
│                                                               │
│    Test Item                                                  │
│                                                               │
│    A symbol in poetry                                         │
│                                                               │
│        *A.  stands for something else.                        │
│         B.  is a simile or metaphor.                          │
│         C.  is easy to understand.                            │
│         D.  appeals to the ear.                               │
├─────────────────────────────────────────────────────────────┤
│    Response Profile                                           │
│        *A    B    C    D      (Alternatives)                  │
│         8    5    6    6      (# of student responses)        │
├─────────────────────────────────────────────────────────────┤
│    Item Difficulty                                            │
│                                                               │
│             Item difficulty = 8/25 = .32                      │
└─────────────────────────────────────────────────────────────┘
```

Example 5.5 shows an item difficulty of .32, indicating a difficult item. According to the response profile, students responded randomly. Ideally, a test should seldom contain items with difficulties below .30.

ITEM DISCRIMINATION

In addition to analyzing the item response profile and calculating the item difficulty, teachers can use a third technique to assess test items. *Item discrimination* provides an index of how an item discriminates between high- and low-scoring students.

Test items can indicate positive, negative, or no discrimination, expressed on a scale from $+1.00$ to -1.00. *Positive discrimination* occurs when more high- than low-scoring students respond correctly to a test item. Maximum positive discrimination occurs when all high-scoring students respond correctly to the item and no low-scoring students succeed on it. The discrimination for such an item would be $+1.00$. *Negative discrimination* occurs when more low- than high-scoring students respond correctly to a test item. Such items often have serious problems and must be revised or discarded. Maximum negative discrimination occurs when all low-scoring students respond correctly to the item and no high-scoring students succeed on it. The discrimination for such an item would be -1.00. This is a rare situation. *No discrimination* occurs when an equal number of high- and low-scoring students respond correctly to a test item. The discrimination for such an item would be 0.00. A test item with no discrimination should be reviewed and in all likelihood rewritten because it does not differentiate between the two groups.

To determine item discrimination, follow these steps:

- Arrange test scores in order from highest to lowest.
- Determine the number of students (K) to use in the high- and low-scoring groups. The number of students who completed the test will determine the percentage of the class to use for K. The following percentages are recommended: K = 50% if 20 or fewer students completed the test, K = 33% if 21 to 39 students completed the test, and K = 25% if 40 or more students completed the test.

- Determine the number of students from the high-scoring group who responded correctly to the test item (H).
- Determine the number of students from the low-scoring group who responded correctly to the test item (L).

Item discrimination is calculated by the following formula:

FORMULA

$$\text{Item discrimination} = \frac{H - L}{K}$$

K = 50% of the class if 20 or fewer students completed the test
K = 33% of the class if 21 to 39 students completed the test
K = 25% of the class if 40 or more students completed the test
H = # of high-scoring students responding correctly to the item
L = # of low-scoring students responding correctly to the item

---

EXAMPLE 5.6

Assume a class of *27 students* (K = 9). The number of students from the high- and low-scoring groups who responded correctly to each item is indicated. Compute the item discrimination index for each of the following test items:

Item	High-scoring	Low-scoring
1.	8	2
2.	3	6
3.	4	4

In Example 5.6, for a class of 27, 9 students (K = 33% of 27 or K = 9) were identified in the high- and low-scoring groups. Item 1 shows that 8 students from the high-scoring group (H = 8) and 2 students from the low-scoring group (L = 2) responded correctly. Item 1 discriminates positively, since more students from the high- than from the low-scoring group responded correctly.

$$\text{Item discrimination} = \frac{H - L}{K}$$

$$\text{Item discrimination} = \frac{8 - 2}{9} = .67$$

Item 2 shows that 3 students from the high-scoring group (H = 3) and 6 students from the low-scoring group (L = 6) responded correctly. Item 2 discriminates negatively, since more students from the low- than from the high-scoring group responded correctly.

$$\text{Item discrimination} = \frac{3 - 6}{9} = -.33$$

Item 3 shows that 4 students from the high-scoring group (H = 4) and 4 students from the low-scoring group (L = 4) responded correctly. Item 3 shows no discrimination, since an equal number of students from both groups responded correctly.

$$\text{Item discrimination} = \frac{4 - 4}{9} = .00$$

EXAMPLE 5.7

Assume a class of *20 students* (K = 10) and compute the item discrimination index for the following test item. Then describe what, if any, action should be taken to revise the item (* indicates correct response).

Test Item

Group	Response Profile				Discrimination Index
	*A	B	C	D	
High	10	0	0	0	$\frac{10 - 3}{10} = .70$
Low	3	2	2	3	
Both	13	2	2	3	

Action to be taken: This is a good item that discriminates positively. No action is necessary.

In example 5.7, for a class of 20, 10 students (K = 50% of 20 or K = 10) were identified in the high- and low-scoring groups. The item shows that 10 students from the high-scoring group (H = 10) and 3 students from the low-scoring group (L = 3) responded correctly. This item discriminates positively, since more high-scoring than low-scoring students responded correctly.

EXAMPLE 5.8

Assume a class of *30 students* (K = 10) and compute the item discrimination index for the following test item. Then describe what, if any, action should be taken to revise the item (* indicates correct response).

Test Item

Group	Response Profile				Discrimination Index
	A	*B	C	D	
High	8	1	0	1	$\frac{1 - 4}{10} = -.30$
Low	3	4	0	3	
Both	11	5	0	4	

Action to be taken: This item is negatively discriminating (more students from the low- than from the high-scoring group responded correctly to it). More high-scoring students responded to distractor A than to the correct alternative. In addition, no high- or low-scoring students responded to alternative C. Rewrite or discard this item.

In example 5.8, for a class of 30, 10 students (K = 33% of 30 or K = 10) were identified in the high- and low-scoring groups. The middle 33 percent (10 students) were not used in calculating item discrimination. The item shows that 1 student from the high-scoring group (H = 1) and 4 students from the low-scoring group (L = 4) responded correctly). This item discriminates negatively, since more low-scoring than high-scoring students responded correctly.

EXAMPLE 5.9

Assume a class of *40 students* (K = 10) and compute the item discrimination index for the following test item. Then describe what, if any, action should be taken to revise the item (* indicates correct response).

Test Item

Group	Response Profile				Discrimination Index
	A	B	C	*D	
High	2	1	0	7	$\dfrac{7-7}{10} = .00$
Low	2	0	1	7	
Both	4	1	1	14	

Action to be taken: This item has no discrimination (an equal number of students from the low- and high-scoring groups responded correctly). Rewrite or discard this item.

In example 5.9, for a class of 40, 10 students (K = 25% of 40 or K = 10) were identified in the high- and low-scoring groups. The middle 50 percent (20 students) were not used in calculating item discrimination. The item shows that 7 students from the high-scoring group (H = 7) and 7 students from the low-scoring group (L = 7) responded correctly. This item has no discrimination since an equal number of students from the high- and low-scoring groups responded correctly.

Many schools have computer software programs that analyze test items and provide response profiles, and also calculate item difficulty and discrimination indexes. See Appendix C for a listing of software resources. Different computer programs use different percentages of students in high- and low-scoring groups to calculate an item discrimination index. The percentages suggested in this publication are based on class size (20 or fewer students = 50%, 21 to 39 students = 33%, 40 or more students = 25%).

After scoring a test, teachers must analyze test items by reviewing response profiles and determining item difficulty and discrimination by hand or by using a computer program. Information about item difficulty and discrimination will assist teachers in writing better test items that will ultimately result in a more accurate assessment of student achievement.

EXAMPLE 5.10

Assume a class of *40 students* (K = 10) and compute the item discrimination index for the following test item. Then describe what, if any, action should be taken to revise the item (* indicates correct response).

Test Item

The design principle that stresses the use of contrasting elements so controlled and placed as to hold and retain attention is

    A. balance.
    B. proportion.
    C. unity.
  *D. variety.

Response Profile

A	B	C	*D	(Alternatives)
4	1	0	5	(# of H responses)
2	7	0	1	(# of L responses)

Item Discrimination

$$\text{Item discrimination} = \frac{5 - 1}{10} = \frac{4}{10} = .40$$

Action to be taken: For a class of 40, 10 students (K = 25% of 40 or K = 10) were identified in the high- and low-scoring groups. The response profile reveals that the correct choice is alternative D and the item discrimination is positive, since 5 high-scoring students and 1 low-scoring student responded correctly. Further examination shows alternative A to be a poor distractor, since it attracted more high- than low-scoring students. Alternative C is ineffective, since it attracted no students from either group. Alternative B is an effective distractor because it attracted more low- than high-scoring students. Replace alternative C and revise alternative A.

EXAMPLE 5.11

Assume a class of *40 students* completed the following test items. Interpret the item difficulty and discrimination indexes for each item.

Item Number	Item Difficulty	Item Discrimination
1	.60	.50
2	.40	.00
3	.20	.30
4	.10	−.10
5	.90	.10

Difficulty of items is interpreted as follows:

- Items 1 and 2: Moderate difficulty (.30 to .70)
- Items 3 and 4: High difficulty (.30 or less)
- Item 5: Low difficulty (.70 or greater).

Discrimination for items is interpreted as follows:

- Item 1: High discrimination (.40 or higher)
- Item 3: Moderate discrimination (.30 to .40)
- Items 2 and 5: Very low discrimination (.20 or less)
- Item 4: Negative discrimination (examine for revision).

REVIEW QUESTIONS AND ACTIVITIES

Questions

1. What is a response profile?

2. What is item difficulty?

3. What is item discrimination?

Activities

1. Assume a class of *20 students* and compute difficulty and discrimination indexes for the following three test items. Then describe what, if any, action should be taken to revise these items (* indicates correct response).

Test Item #1

Group	A	B	C	*D	Difficulty Index	Discrimination Index
High	6	2	0	2		
Low	0	2	0	8		
Both	6	4	0	10		

Action to be taken for item #1:

Test Item #2

Group	Response Profile				Difficulty Index	Discrimination Index
	A	B	*C	D		
High	1	0	8	1		
Low	3	2	3	2		
Both	4	2	11	3		

Action to be taken for item #2:

Test Item #3

Group	Response Profile				Difficulty Index	Discrimination Index
	*A	B	C	D		
High	5	0	0	5		
Low	2	0	5	3		
Both	7	0	5	8		

Action to be taken for item #3:

Chapter 6

IMPROVING TEST VALIDITY AND RELIABILITY

Classroom tests should provide valid and reliable measures of student performance. An understanding of the procedures used to determine validity and reliability is necessary to assess the test as a whole.

VALIDITY

Validity is the extent to which a test measures what it was intended to measure. It is the most important requisite of any test. Even if other practical and technical considerations are satisfactory, the test's quality is doubtful without supportive evidence of validity.

The four major types of validity used with teacher-made tests are content, construct, concurrent, and predictive. Each type requires a specific procedure and has a primary use.

EXAMPLE 6.1

Types of Test Validity

Type	*Procedure*	*Primary use*
Content	Compares test items with instructional objectives	Assessment of content
Construct	Identifies underlying concepts measured by test	Assessment of adequacy
Concurrent	Compares test with a similar measure of present performance	Provision of substitute test for less convenient existing measure
Predictive	Compares test performance with future outcome	Selection and classification of students

---

Content Validity

Content validity is the most common type of validation teachers use to ascertain if the test provides an accurate assessment of the instructional objectives. No empirical procedures are used to establish content validity. Rather, test items are individually analyzed and compared with the levels of behavior specified in the instructional objectives.

Teachers attempting to establish content validity should consult a reading level word list—a published list that indicates an average student's reading level for a specific age or grade. Such a checking device can ensure that the vocabulary used in the test item is not an obstacle to students.

Construct Validity

Construct validity identifies the psychological traits or underlying constructs of a test. Constructs are hypothetical qualities that are assumed to exist in order to account for behavior in varying situations. Essentially, this type of validity asks the question, "What is the test actually measuring?" For example, in a test developed to measure a mentally retarded student's ability to use metric linear concepts (Example 6.2), the constructs might consist of (1) assigning and recognizing metric symbols, (2) assigning and recognizing metric values, (3) associative conceptualization of scale numbers to measurement lengths, (4) psychomotor ability to measure objects with a metric scale and conceptualize with length measurements, and (5) test-taking ability that would include the following:

- Attention span
- Familiarity with mechanics of test (following directions, etc.)
- Test-wise ability (experience in test taking)
- Transferability of answers to response sheet.

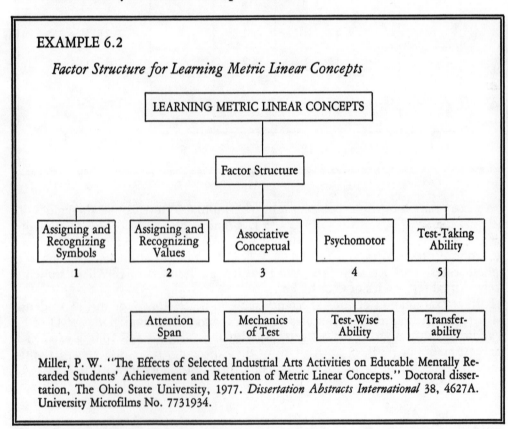

EXAMPLE 6.2

Factor Structure for Learning Metric Linear Concepts

Miller, P. W. "The Effects of Selected Industrial Arts Activities on Educable Mentally Retarded Students' Achievement and Retention of Metric Linear Concepts." Doctoral dissertation, The Ohio State University, 1977. *Dissertation Abstracts International* 38, 4627A. University Microfilms No. 7731934.

Concurrent Validity

Concurrent validity compares a teacher-made test with a similar assessment measure. A major reason for establishing concurrent validity is to substitute a test for a more time-consuming or more complex instrument.

Predictive Validity

Predictive validity compares test performance with a future outcome—for example, using ninth grade Scholastic Aptitude Test scores to predict success in tenth grade high school chemistry. Both concurrent and predictive validity rely on correlation coefficients or an expectancy table to indicate the degree of relationship.

Suppose a teacher is interested in determining the usefulness of a mathematics aptitude test (administered at the beginning of the school year) to predict final test grades in Algebra I. To determine if the two measures are related, the teacher prepares an expectancy table.

EXAMPLE 6.3

Expectancy Table

Mathematics Aptitude Test Scores and
Final Test Grades in Algebra I

| Mathematics Aptitude Test Scores | | | | | Test Grades |
2–5	6–9	10–13	14–17	18–21	
		1	3	3	7 A's
		10	1	4	15 B's
	4	6	2	1	13 C's
	4	1			5 D's
1	3				4 F's
1	11	18	6	8	44

An examination of this expectancy table (Example 6.3) reveals that the grades on the final test are 7 A's, 15 B's, 13 C's, 5 D's, and 4 F's. Eight of the 44 students had the highest mathematics aptitude test scores (between 18 and 21); six students had aptitude test scores between 14 and 17. Of these 14 students receiving the highest scores, 11 (79 percent) received final test grades of A or B. All 14 students received final test grades of C or higher.

Further examination of the expectancy table indicates that 7 of the 11 students (64 percent) with aptitude test scores between 6 and 9 had final grades of D or F. In addition, 31 of 32 students (97 percent) with aptitude scores of 10 or greater had final test grades of A, B, or C. Analysis of the expectancy table indicates that aptitude test scores would be useful in predicting final test grades in Algebra I.

RELIABILITY

Reliability provides an estimate of the consistency of test results; it is expressed as a correlation coefficient reported on a scale ranging from 0.00 to 1.00. Next to validity, reliability is the most important characteristic of a test. Without reliability, little confidence should be placed in test results. A test that is not valid, but highly reliable, may measure something irrelevant with great precision. Teachers should not, however, expect test results to be perfectly consistent. As a test is administered to different students and/or groups, variations in test scores should be expected because of factors other than quality (for example, fatigue, guessing). Generally, however, if reliability is high, a second administration of a similar test to the same students should produce similar scores. If reliability is low, it is doubtful that two administrations of the same test would produce similar scores.

Reliability coefficients used with teacher-made tests are usually identified by the method used to calculate reliability. These methods are test-retest, equivalent forms, split-half, and Kuder-Richardson Formula 21. Each method follows specific procedures and provides evidence of consistency.

EXAMPLE 6.4

Types of Test Reliability

Method	Procedure	Consistency
Test-Retest	Correlate scores for two administrations of same test. Second administration at later time (i.e., one month, one-half year).	Stability of test results over time
Equivalent Forms	Correlate scores for two forms of test.	Equivalency of forms
Split-Half	Correlate scores for two halves of test. Apply correction formula.	Internal test consistency
Kuder-Richardson Formula 21	Calculate mean and standard deviation of test scores. Compute reliability coefficient.	Internal test consistency

---

Test-Retest

Test-retest is a method of establishing reliability by correlating scores from two administrations of the same test to the same group of students in a given time interval. The interval may vary from a few days to several months, depending on the use of the results. If the results show the students' scores were approximately the same on both administrations of the test, then a positive relationship would exist (1.00 indicates a perfect positive relationship; 0.00 indicates no relationship). This method is seldom used to establish reliability for teacher-made tests because of the requirement of administering the test twice to the same students.

Equivalent Forms

Equivalent forms is a method of establishing reliability by correlating scores from two different, but equivalent, forms of a test. The two tests are administered to the same students and the scores are correlated. The correlation provides an estimate of how well both forms of the test assess the same instructional objectives. This method is seldom used to determine reliability of teacher-made tests because of the requirement of two forms of the same test and two testing sessions.

Split-Half

Split-half is a method of establishing reliability by correlating the scores from two halves of the same test. Usually the scores from the odd- and even-numbered test items are correlated. The correlation coefficient provides a measure of internal consistency and indicates the equivalency of the two halves in assessing the instructional objectives. Finally, a correction formula (Spearman-Brown) is applied to the correlation coefficient, which establishes a reliability coefficient for the entire test.

FORMULA

Spearman-Brown Formula

$$\text{Reliability of entire test} = \frac{2 \times \text{Reliability on } \frac{1}{2} \text{ test}}{1 + \text{Reliability on } \frac{1}{2} \text{ test}}$$

If, for example, the half-tests correlated .50, then the correlation coefficient of the whole test would be .67.

EXAMPLE 6.5

$$\text{Reliability of entire test} = \frac{2 \times .50}{1 + .50} = \frac{1.00}{1.50} = .67$$

Kuder-Richardson Formula 21

The *Kuder-Richardson Formula 21 (KR21)* is a method of establishing reliability that requires a single administration of a test and uses the mean and standard deviation of the test scores.

FORMULA

Kuder-Richardson Formula 21 (KR21)

$$KR21 = \frac{A}{A - 1} \left(1 - \frac{\overline{X}(A - \overline{X})}{A\,(SD)^2} \right)$$

A = test length (# of items)

$\overline{X}$ = mean of the test scores

SD = standard deviation of the test scores

If, for example, a distribution of test scores for a 50-item test has a mean of 30 and a standard deviation of 6, the KR21 reliability is .68.

EXAMPLE 6.6

$$KR21 = \frac{50}{49} \left(1 - \frac{30\,(50 - 30)}{50\,(6)^2} \right) = .68$$

The KR21 is easily determined if the mean and standard deviation of the test scores have previously been calculated. This can be done with a hand-held calculator or one of several statistic software programs used with microcomputers.

Improving Test Reliability

Several test characteristics affect reliability. They include the following:

- *Test length*. In general, a longer test is more reliable than a shorter one because longer tests sample the instructional objectives more adequately. Considering this single factor, teachers should strive for longer tests whenever circumstances permit.
- *Spread of scores*. The type of students taking the test can influence reliability. A group of students with heterogeneous ability will produce a larger spread of test scores than will a group with homogeneous ability.
- *Item difficulty*. In general, tests composed of items of moderate difficulty (.30 to .70) will have more influence on reliability than those composed mainly of easy or difficult items.
- *Item discrimination*. In general, tests composed of more discriminating items will have greater reliability than those composed of less discriminating items.
- *Time limits*. Adding a time factor may improve reliability for lower-level cognitive test items. Since all students do not function at the same pace, a time factor adds another criterion to the test that causes discrimination, thus improving reliability. Teachers should not, however, arbitrarily impose a time limit. For higher-level cognitive test items, the imposition of a time limit may defeat the intended purpose of the items.

REVIEW QUESTIONS AND ACTIVITIES

Questions

1. When several people correct and score a test with the same results, it is
   - A. reliable.
   - B. valid.
   - C. comprehensive.
   - D. objective.

2. When a test measures what it is intended to measure, it is
   - A. reliable.
   - B. valid.
   - C. comprehensive.
   - D. objective.

3. When a test is a consistent measure of student achievement, it is
   - A. reliable.
   - B. valid.
   - C. comprehensive.
   - D. objective.

4. Reliability is to validity as
   - A. content is to construct.
   - B. accuracy is to error.
   - C. consistency is to truth.
   - D. precision is to flexibility.

5. The story in which the size of the fish that was caught gets bigger and bigger is an example of good or bad
     A. reliability.
     B. validity.
     C. objectivity.
     D. comprehensiveness.

Activities

1. Describe the procedures used to demonstrate content validity.

2. Describe the procedures used to demonstrate predictive validity.

3. Describe the procedures used to demonstrate test-retest reliability.

4. Describe the procedures used to demonstrate split-half reliability.

5. Describe five test characteristics that affect reliability.

APPENDIXES

A. HIERARCHICAL LEVELS OF THE LEARNING DOMAINS

*Affective Domain**

1. Receiving
   Becomes aware; is willing to learn and try a particular response.

2. Responding
   Initially may react out of compliance, later out of willingness/satisfaction.
   (Requires Receiving)

3. Valuing
   The process of accepting the worth of an object, idea, or behavior, attempting to promote it as a value; and developing commitment.
   (Requires Receiving and Responding)

4. Organization
   Determining interrelationships of values; establishing a hierarchy.
   (Requires Receiving, Responding, and Valuing)

5. Characterization by a Value Complex
   Generalizing selected values into controlling tendencies with subsequent integration into total philosophy.
   (Requires Receiving, Responding, Valuing, and Organization)

*Cognitive Domain***

1. Knowledge
   Ability to define terms, recall customs, traditions, trends, classifications, categories, criteria, principles, generalizations.

2. Comprehension
   Ability to explain, describe, illustrate, summarize, interpret, note consequences of ideas, procedures or methods.
   (Requires Knowledge)

3. Application
   Ability to apply or use ideas, procedures, methods.
   (Requires Knowledge and Comprehension)

4. Analysis
   Ability to break down, compare, contrast, distinguish between, perceive, analyze ideas into constituent parts.
   (Requires Knowledge, Comprehension, and Application)

5. Synthesis
   Ability to put together, create, plan, develop, make, produce, recommend, generalize, formulate a new idea, procedure or method.
   (Requires Knowledge, Comprehension, Application, and Analysis)

6. Evaluation
   Ability to evaluate, assess the value of ideas, methods, using appropriate criteria.
   (Requires Knowledge, Comprehension, Application, Analysis, and Synthesis)

---

*Krathwohl, D. R.; Bloom, B. S.; and Masia, B. B. *Taxonomy of Educational Objectives: Handbook II, Affective Domain*. New York: David McKay, 1964.
**Bloom, B. S.; Englehart, M. D.; Furst, E. J.; Hill, W. H.; and Krathwohl, D. R. *Taxonomy of Educational Objectives: Handbook I, Cognitive Domain*. New York: David McKay, 1956.

Psychomotor Domain

1. Perception
   Become aware through sense organs. Recognize cues, make choices, and relate to actions.

2. Set
   Mental, physical, or emotional readiness.
   (Requires Perception)

3. Guided Response
   Overt actions by limitation and/or trial and error under supervision.
   (Requires Perception and Set)

4. Mechanism
   Habitual response.
   (Requires Perception, Set, and Guided Response)

5. Complex Overt Response
   Action performed without hesitation, leading to automatic performance.
   (Requires Perception, Set, Guided Response, and Mechanism)

6. Adaptation
   Altering activities to fit new situations.
   (Requires Perception, Set, Guided Response, Mechanism, and Complex Overt Response)

7. Origination
   Creating new actions to fit a situation.
   (Requires Perception, Set, Guided Response, Mechanism, Complex Overt Response, and Adaptation)

Simpson, E. J. "The Classification of Educational Objectives in the Psychomotor Domain." *The Psychomotor Domain*. Vol. 3. Washington, D.C.: Gryphon House, 1972.

B. SAMPLE VERBS FOR WRITING INSTRUCTIONAL OBJECTIVES

Sample Verbs Used to Identify Specific Student Behaviors

General Discriminative Behaviors

Choose	Describe	Discriminate	Indicate	Match	Place
Collect	Detect	Distinguish	Isolate	Omit	Point
Define	Differentiate	Identify	List	Order	Select

Study Behaviors

Arrange	Classify	Follow	Look	Organize	Sort
Categorize	Compile	Formulate	Map	Quote	Underline
Chart	Copy	Gather	Mark	Record	
Cite	Diagram	Itemize	Name	Reproduce	
Circle	Document	Label	Note	Search	

Analysis Behaviors

Analyze	Compare	Criticize	Evaluate	Generate	Plan
Appraise	Conclude	Deduce	Explain	Induce	Structure
Combine	Contrast	Defend	Formulate	Infer	

Creative Behaviors

Alter	Generalize	Rearrange	Rename	Restructure	Simplify
Ask	Paraphrase	Recombine	Reorder	Retell	Synthesize
Change	Predict	Reconstruct	Rephrase	Rewrite	Systematize
Design	Question	Regroup	Restate		

Miscellaneous Behaviors

Attempt	Discover	Grind	Position	Send	Suggest
Attend	Distribute	Hold	Present	Serve	Supply
Begin	End	Include	Produce	Sew	Support
Bring	Erase	Inform	Propose	Share	Switch
Buy	Expand	Lead	Provide	Sharpen	Take
Complete	Extend	Lend	Put	Shorten	Tear
Consider	Find	Light	Raise	Shut	Touch
Correct	Finish	Make	Relate	Signify	Type
Crush	Fit	Mend	Repeat	Start	Use
Designate	Fix	Miss	Return	Store	Vote
Develop	Get	Offer	Save	Strike	

Claus, C. K. ''Verbs and Imperative Sentences as a Basis for Stating Educational Objectives.'' Paper given at the meeting of the National Council on Measurement in Education, Chicago, 1968.

Sample Verbs Used in Various Curriculum Areas

Art Behaviors

Assemble	Construct	Illustrate	Mold	Pour	Sculpt
Carve	Draw	Melt	Paint	Press	Sketch
Color	Fold	Mix	Paste	Roll	Trace

Drama Behaviors

Cross	Display	Exit	Move	Pass	Sit
Direct	Enter	Leave	Pantomime	Proceed	Turn

Language Behaviors

Accent	Hyphenate	Pronounce	Speak	Summarize	Verbalize
Alphabetize	Indent	Punctuate	Spell	Syllabicate	Whisper
Edit	Outline	Read	State	Translate	Write

Laboratory Science Behaviors

Calibrate	Convert	Dissect	Increase	Manipulate	Report
Conduct	Decrease	Feed	Lengthen	Prepare	Specify
Connect	Demonstrate	Grow	Limit	Remove	Weigh

Mathematical Behaviors

Add	Divide	Graph	Interpolate	Prove	Square
Bisect	Estimate	Group	Measure	Reduce	Tabulate
Calculate	Extrapolate	Integrate	Multiply	Solve	Verify

Music Behaviors

Blow	Compose	Hum	Pluck	Sing	Tap
Bow	Finger	Mute	Practice	Strum	Whistle
Clap	Harmonize	Play			

Physical Behaviors

Bend	Hit	Kick	Run	Somersault	Swing
Catch	Hop	March	Skate	Stretch	Throw
Grasp	Jump	Pitch	Skip	Swim	Walk

Social Behaviors

Agree	Compliment	Disagree	Greet	Join	Participate
Answer	Contribute	Discuss	Help	Laugh	Praise
Argue	Cooperate	Forgive	Invite	Meet	Smile

Claus, C. K. "Verbs and Imperative Sentences as a Basis for Stating Educational Objectives." Paper given at the meeting of the National Council on Measurement in Education, Chicago, 1968.

LRX Test (test-generation program)
Logic Extension Resources
9651 Business Center Drive, Suite C
Rancho Cucamonga, CA 91730
(714) 980–0046

MicroGrade (grade-keeping program)
Chariot Software Group
3659 India Street, Suite 100
San Diego, CA 92103
1–800–242–7468

MicroTest II (test-generation program)
Chariot Software Group
3659 India Street, Suite 100
San Diego, CA 92103
1–800–242–7468

Score (test-scoring program)
Flagstaff Engineering
1120 Kaibab Lane
Flagstaff, AZ 86001
(602) 779–3341

Teacher's Aide (test-generation program)
Jensen Enterprises, Inc.
2979 Pershing Drive
Coloma, MI 49038
(616) 849–2753

Test Quest (test-generation program)
Allen Communication
5225 Wiley Post Way
Salt Lake City, UT 84116
(801) 537–7800

D. SAMPLE TEST ITEMS

This appendix presents sample test items from art, biology, chemistry, English, French, home economics, industrial education, mathematics, music, physical education, physics, science, social studies, and Spanish. These test items were contributed by practicing teachers and organized by the authors to provide a consistent format.

ART

True-False Items

__T__ 1. Gauguin is best known for paintings of South Sea islanders.

__F__ 2. Complementary colors mixed together become brighter.

__T__ 3. Degas painted and drew ballet dancers.

__F__ 4. A 4-B drawing pencil has hard lead.

__T__ 5. Toulouse-Lautrec made posters to advertise entertainers.

Multiple-Choice Items

1. An etching is an example of
    A. relief printing.
   *B. intaglio printing.
    C. lithographic printing.
    D. gravure printing.

2. What artist is known for a series of paintings of the same subject in different lights?
    A. Picasso
    B. Manet
   *C. Monet
    D. Rembrandt

3. What artist made scientific drawings during the Renaissance period?
    A. Van Gogh
    B. Rubens
    C. Michelangelo
   *D. da Vinci

4. What artist is known for dripping paint on canvas?
   *A. Pollock
    B. Cezanne
    C. Van Gogh
    D. Seurat

5. Impressionists were a group of artists who usually
   *A. painted nature out-of-doors.
    B. painted still life in studios.
    C. made impressions from wood blocks.
    D. used dreams for subject matter.

Matching Items

	I		II
E	1. used for paste-ups	A.	turpentine
C	2. used for painting or drawing in color	B.	water
G	3. applied to canvas before oil painting	C.	pastels
A	4. mixed with oil paints	D.	palette
D	5. board used to mix paints	E.	rubber cement
		F.	shellac
		G.	gesso

Essay Item

Define *line, volume, shape, texture, value,* and *color* and describe how each design element is used in a drawing.

Points for grading

- Design elements are defined (6 points).
- Description is provided concerning how each design element is used in a drawing (6 points).

Sample test items were prepared by Ray Schultz, former art teacher, Cape May County Vocational Schools, Cape May Court House, NJ.

BIOLOGY

True-False Items

__F__ 1. Plants are capable of losing water by the process of *dehydration* through the vascular bundles.

__T__ 2. Diseases are changes from the normal state that prevent specific organs from carrying out their functions.

__F__ 3. A substance that releases hydroxyl ions when dissolved in water or that can give off protons when reacting chemically is a base.

__T__ 4. During the dark stage of photosynthesis, the energy produced during the light phase is converted into sugar and oxygen through chemical reactions that do not involve light.

__T__ 5. A catalyst is a substance that stimulates the occurrence of a chemical reaction by lowering the activation energy requirement and that does not become a part of the final product.

Multiple-Choice Items

1. A basic determiner of heredity is
   A. amino acid.
   *B. DNA.
   C. mutation.
   D. RNA.

2. An example of an inherited gene mutation in humans is
   A. exposure to radiation.
   B. replication of DNA.
   *C. sickle-cell anemia.
   D. synthesis of proteins.

3. A peptide bond forms between
   *A. the carboxyl group of one amino acid and the amino group of another amino acid.
   B. the carboxyl groups of two amino acids.
   C. two amino acids with the addition of a water molecule.
   D. an amino acid and a carbohydrate with the loss of a water molecule.

4. The probability of a family having a girl and two boys in that order is
   A. one-third.
   B. one-half.
   C. one-sixth.
   *D. one-eighth.

The following diagram represents a trait for albinism. Individuals who are albinos are represented by filled-in circles.

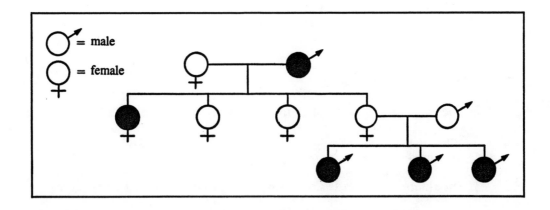

5. From studying the preceding diagram, one can determine that albinism
   *A. is a recessive trait.
   B. is a dominant trait.
   C. affects only men.
   D. is passed on by only one parent.

Matching Items

	I		II
E	1. hemophilia	A.	autosome dominant
B	2. sickle-cell anemia and cystic fibrosis	B.	autosome recessive
D	3. Down's syndrome	C.	polyfactorial
		D.	trisomy
		E.	X-linked recessive gene

Essay Item

Each year thousands of salmon return to the same freshwater spawning area where they had their beginning. How they know where to go is still a mystery. One suggestion is that hormones found in the cells of the salmon affect the existing osmotic conditions between the cells and the surrounding sea water. It is possible that the hormones secreted in the cells of the fish are synchronized with spawning. Discuss spawning migration in terms of existing osmotic conditions and the secretion of specific hormones.

Points for grading

- Relating answer to general comments about osmosis (2 points).
- Relating osmosis to the conditions between salmon and sea water (3 points).

Sample test items were prepared by James Kelly, Malcolm Price Laboratory School, University of Northern Iowa, Cedar Falls.

CHEMISTRY

True-False Items

T   1. The chemical behaviors of sodium and cesium are similar.

F   2. Since an atom is electrically neutral, the number of protons is equal to the number of neutrons.

F   3. The chloride ion consists of 17 protons, 18 neutrons, and 18 electrons.

T   4. The algebraic sum of the oxidation numbers of the atoms in the formula of a compound is zero.

T   5. A covalent bond is formed in the diatomic hydrogen molecule.

T   6. The oxidation number for magnesium and barium is 2+.

F   7. Since an atom is electrically neutral, the number of electrons is equal to the number of neutrons.

F   8. The sodium ion consists of 11 protons, 11 electrons, and 12 neutrons.

T   9. The oxidation number of chlorine in potassium chlorate ($KClO_3$) is 5+.

T   10. A double covalent bond is formed in diatomic oxygen.

Multiple-Choice Items

1. A vertical column of elements in the periodic table is a/an
      *A. family.
      B. octet.
      C. period.
      D. series.

2. The element capable of replacing all others in the halogen family is
      A. bromine.
      B. chlorine.
      *C. fluorine.
      D. iodine.

3. The oxidation number of phosphorous in the polyatomic ion PO_4^{3-} is
      A. 3+
      *B. 5+
      C. 2+
      D. 4+

4. The number of moles of aluminum atoms reacting with three moles of oxygen molecules in the equation $4Al + 3O_2 \rightarrow 2Al_2O_3$ is
      A. 1
      B. 2
      C. 3
      *D. 4

5. The number of moles in one kilogram of zinc is
   A. 14.1
   *B. 15.1
   C. 16.5
   D. 33.3

6. A horizontal row of elements in the periodic table from sodium to argon is a/an
   A. family.
   B. octet.
   *C. series.
   D. group.

7. The oxidation number of sulfur in the polyatomic ion SO_4^{2-} is
   A. 2+
   B. 4+
   *C. 6+
   D. 8+

8. The number of grams in 2.5 moles of carbon dioxide is
   A. 28
   B. 44
   C. 88
   *D. 110

9. The number of moles of oxygen atoms reacting with four moles of aluminum atoms in the equation $4Al + 3O_2 \rightarrow 2Al_2O_3$ is
   A. 2
   B. 4
   *C. 6
   D. 8

10. The molarity of a solution containing 20.0 grams of sodium hydroxide dissolved in 250.0 ml of water is
    *A. 2.0
    B. 1.0
    C. 0.5
    D. 0.25

Matching Items

	I		II
G	1. a substance that does the dissolving	A.	distillation
B	2. two liquids that do not dissolve in each other	B.	immiscible
D	3. a substance of low solubility	C.	miscible
A	4. a method of purifying a substance	D.	precipitate
F	5. the substance being dissolved	E.	soluble
		F.	solute
		G.	solvent

Essay Items (Problems)

In the equation $2NaClO_3 \rightarrow 2NaCl + 3O_2$, how many grams of $NaClO_3$ are required to produce one mole of O_2?

Points for grading

- Answer: 70.7g (3 points)

In the equation $2HCl + CaCO_3 \rightarrow CO_2 + CaCl_2 + H_2O$, how many grams of $CaCO_3$ are required to produce two moles of CO_2?

Points for grading

- Answer: 100 g (3 points)

How many grams of O_2 are needed to react with an excess of C_4H_{10} to produce 5 moles of H_2O?

Points for grading

- Answer: 208 g (3 points)

Sample test items were prepared by Norman E. Anderson, Cedar Falls High School, Iowa.

ENGLISH

True-False Items

F 1. The setting for Shakespeare's *Romeo and Juliet* is 16th century England.

T 2. "Star-crossed lovers" means it was Romeo and Juliet's fate to die.

T 3. Benvolio is the peacemaker in the play.

F 4. Romeo received a formal invitation to the masked feast.

F 5. Paris was at the tomb to give Juliet her wedding ring.

F 6. Romeo was sentenced to death because this is what the prince had decreed.

T 7. A tragedy is a literary work in which the central character meets a disastrous end.

F 8. "Is now the two hours' traffic of our stage ..." is an example of a pun.

Multiple-Choice Items

1. Tybalt's personality trait is described by Mercutio as being like a/an
   A. dog.
   *B. cat.
   C. elephant.
   D. horse.

2. In the Shakespearean plot structure, background information is revealed in the
   *A. exposition.
   B. complication.
   C. climax.
   D. resolution.

3. A long uninterrupted speech while other characters are on stage is a/an
   A. aside.
   B. soliloquy.
   C. couplet.
   *D. monologue.

4. According to Shakespearean plot structure, the climax of this play occurs when
   *A. Tybalt dies.
   B. Romeo dies.
   C. Juliet dies.
   D. Romeo and Juliet marry.

5. Why were the Montagues and Capulets feuding?
   A. Lord Montague once loved Lady Capulet.
   B. Romeo loved Juliet.
   C. Lord Montague cheated Lord Capulet in business.
   *D. Shakespeare does not explain.

6. Before taking the potion, what was Juliet's fear?
   A. It was a poison.
   B. She would regain consciousness alone in the tomb.
   C. She would see and hear her dead kinsmen.
   *D. All of the above.

7. "For never was a story of more woe / Than this of Juliet for her Romeo." This is an example of a
    A. blank verse.
    *B. rhyme couplet.
    C. pun.
    D. prologue.

Matching Items

	I		II
E	1. Juliet's gift of love to Romeo	A.	gold statue
H	2. Romeo's real antagonist	B.	scenery
A	3. Lord Montague's gift to Juliet's memory	C.	wedding flowers
C	4. Paris's gift at the tomb	D.	rope ladder
B	5. backgrounds on a stage that are not easily moved by hand	E.	ring
D	6. Nurse brings to Romeo after the marriage	F.	Mercutio
F	7. Romeo's best friend	G.	letter
I	8. movable item on stage	H.	fate
		I.	prop
		J.	Tybalt

Essay Items

Write a dialogue between the ghosts of Romeo and Juliet. Have them discuss their feelings toward Friar Laurence, Prince Escalus, and the Nurse. Also have them describe how they wish to be remembered.

Points for grading

- Dialogue grammar, punctuation, and format (5 points).
- Attitudes toward Friar Laurence, Prince Escalus, and the Nurse (30 points).
- How they wish to be remembered (5 points).

Write a news obituary for Romeo *or* Juliet. Explain the details of their death, describe two of their best personality traits, and conclude with a list of 10 of their survivors or those who preceded them in death and how they are related. (Remember they were married, so the relationships are more complex at the end of the play than at the beginning.)

Points for grading

- Obituary grammar, punctuation, and format (5 points).
- Details of death (5 points).
- Two of their best personality traits (10 points).
- Ten survivors or those preceding them in death and how they are related (20 points).

Sample test items were prepared by Francie Blaney, former English teacher, Calumet High School, Gary, Indiana, and consultant for the Indiana Writing Project.

FRENCH

True-False Items

__T__ 1. Voici un livre.
(Here is a book.)

__F__ 2. Voici une maison.
(Here is a house.)

Read the following French passage and answer the questions.

Les parents de Pierre ne se sont pas levés aujourd'hui parce qu'ils se sont couchés très tard hier soir après leur surprise-party. Quelle chance pour eux parce que c'est samedi et M. Dubois n'a pas besoin d'aller au bureau.

(Pierre's parents did not get up early today because they went to bed very late last night after their party. What luck for them because it is Saturday and Mr. Dubois does not need to go to the office.)

__T__ 3. Les parents de Pierre sont encore couchés au lit. (Pierre's parents are still in bed.)

__F__ 4. Ils doivent travailler aujourd'hui. (They have to work today.)

__F__ 5. C'est samedi et il y a une surprise-party ce soir. (It is Saturday and there is a party tonight.)

Multiple-Choice Items

Read the following French passage and answer the questions.

Madame Dupont est à la maison. Ce soir elle a décidé de préparer de la soupe à l'oignon pour le dîner. Ce matin elle a acheté des oignons au marché et maintenant elle va préparer cette soupe délicieuse pour sa famille. Toute sa famille aime la soupe à l'oignon sauf son fils Jean-Luc. Sans doute il va manger des frites et un hot dog au lieu de cette soupe.

(Mrs. Dupont is at home. She has decided to make onion soup for dinner this evening. She bought some onions at the market this morning and is now going to prepare this delicious soup for her family. The whole family likes onion soup except her son Jean-Luc. No doubt he will eat French fries and a hot dog instead of the soup.)

---

1. Où est Madame Dupont? (Where is Mrs. Dupont?)

    A. Elle est au marché. (She is at the market.)
    B. Elle est à table. (She is at the table.)
  *C. Elle est chez elle. (She is at home.)
    D. Elle est dans la cuisine. (She is in the kitchen.)

2. Qu' est-ce qu'elle va préparer ce soir? (What is she going to prepare tonight?)

    *A. De la soupe à l'oignon. (Onion soup)
    B. Des frites. (French fries)
    C. Des hots dogs. (Hot dogs)
    D. Un hot dog délicieux. (A delicious hot dog)

3. Est-ce que toute la famille aime cette soupe? (Does everyone like this soup?)

    A. Oui, tout le monde l'aime. (Yes, everyone likes it.)
    B. Oui, mais pas son mari. (Yes, but not her husband.)
    *C. Non, pas son fils. (No, not her son.)
    D. Non, sa fille ne l'aime pas beaucoup. (No, her daughter does not like it much.)

Essay Items

Describe in French a typical family meal at your house.

Points for grading

- Proper spelling and use of food and drink items (5 points).
- Good composition (5 points).

Describe in French an incident in your life when you were young. Be sure to pay special attention to the use of the imperfect and the past definite tenses. Include how the incident happened, where, why, and the consequences. This essay should be at least one page in length.

Points for grading

- The incident includes proper imperfect and past definite tenses (10 points).
- The incident identifies the how, where, why, and the consequences (10 points).
- The essay is at least one page in length (5 points).

Sample test items were prepared by James E. Becker, Modern Language Department, Malcolm Price Laboratory School, University of Northern Iowa, Cedar Falls.

HOME ECONOMICS

True-False Items

T 1. Cottage cheese, yogurt, and ice cream are examples of choices from the milk group of the basic four food groups.

F 2. Peanut butter, whole wheat bread, and ground beef are included in the meat group.

T 3. One medium whole fruit or one-half cup of cooked vegetables equals one serving from the fruit/vegetable group.

T 4. Citrus fruits include oranges, grapefruit, and tangerines.

T 5. Four or more daily servings of foods from the bread and cereal group are needed.

Multiple-Choice Items

1. Which is a synthetic fiber?
    A. cotton
    B. linen
    C. alpaca
    *D. polyester

2. Fabrics that use the twill weave are
    *A. denim and gabardine.
    B. gabardine and nylon.
    C. gingham and nylon.
    D. nylon and linen.

3. Which is a type of sleeve?
    A. mandarin
    B. Peter Pan
    *C. raglan
    D. shawl

4. Lines used in clothing design to create a feeling of height and slimness are
    A. diagonal.
    B. horizontal.
    *C. vertical.
    D. curvy.

5. A natural fiber is
    A. acrylic.
    B. rayon.
    C. triacetate.
    *D. wool.

Matching Items

	I		II
G	1. processing method for low acid foods		A. blanching
B	2. processing method for high acid foods		B. boiling water bath
E	3. meats and vegetables		C. high acid foods
F	4. canning method recommended only for jellies		D. hot pack
C	5. fruits, pickles, tomatoes		E. low acid foods
			F. open kettle method
			G. pressure cooker
			H. raw or cold pack

Essay Items

Explain the procedure for preparing a basic white sauce. Include ingredients and three or more uses.

Points for grading

- Procedure is clear and understandable (8 points).
- Ingredients are correctly stated (6 points).
- Three or more uses are given (6 points).

Prepare a personal monthly budget, providing specific examples of fixed and flexible expenses.

Points for grading

- Budget is clear, accurate, and understandable (10 points).
- Specific examples are provided for fixed and flexible expenses (10 points).

Sample test items were prepared by Judith M. Tucker, Bettsville Local Schools, Ohio.

INDUSTRIAL EDUCATION

True-False Items

T   1. A #4 wood screw is smaller in diameter than a #10 wood screw.

F   2. An abrasive paper grit size 120 is coarser than an abrasive paper grit size 80.

F   3. Plywood, particle board, and hardboard are purchased by board feet.

T   4. An 8d nail is 2½'' long.

F   5. An auger bit stamped 12 on the tang would bore a hole 7/8''.

Multiple-Choice Items

1. A process of hammering and squeezing metal (usually heated) into a required shape is
    A. casting.
    B. extruding.
    *C. forging.
    D. machining.

2. A metal casting process that produces a very fine finish is
    A. centrifugal.
    B. full mold.
    C. green sand.
    *D. investment.

3. The slot that is made in wood when sawing is the
    A. groove.
    *B. kerf.
    C. kreft.
    D. rake.

4. The two methods of drying lumber are air drying and
    A. age drying.
    B. chemical drying.
    C. evaporation drying.
    *D. kiln drying.

5. The solvent for shellac is
    *A. alcohol.
    B. lacquer thinner.
    C. turpentine.
    D. water.

Matching Items

	I		II
D	1.		A. cove
F	2.		B. lock dado
A	3.		C. miter
E	4.		D. nosing
			E. ogee
			F. quarter-round

Essay Item

Describe the difference between continuous and intermittent manufacturing. Provide three examples of products produced by each of these manufacturing processes.

Points for grading
- Key words (*continuous* and *intermittent*) are defined (10 points).
- Three product examples for continuous manufacturing are given (10 points).
- Three product examples for intermittent manufacturing are given (10 points).

Sample test items were prepared by Duane H. Rippe, Holmes Junior High School, Cedar Falls, Iowa.

MATHEMATICS

True-False Items

_F_ 1. For every positive number x, $\sqrt{x}$ is less than x.

_T_ 2. The expression $3x - 2 - 2(3x - 7)$ is equal to $-3x + 12$.

_T_ 3. The product $(3a + 5)(a - 1)$ equals $3a^2 + 2a - 5$.

_F_ 4. If triangle ABC is isosceles and the measure of angle A is 100°, then B is 100°.

_F_ 5. Seven is a factor of 17.

Multiple-Choice Items

1. The diameter of one circle is 6 cm and the diameter of another circle is 12 cm. How many cm larger is the area of one circle than the other?
   - A. 3π cm²
   - B. 6π cm²
   - *C. 27π cm²
   - D. 108π cm²

2. A heptagon has how many sides?
   - A. 5
   - B. 6
   - *C. 7
   - D. 8

3. What is the expanded product of $(2x - 4)$ and $(x + 1)$?
   - A. $2x^2 - 4$
   - B. $2x^2 + 4$
   - C. $2x^2 + 2x + 4$
   - *D. $2x^2 - 2x - 4$

4. If $9 - a = 0.5a$, what does a equal?
   - A. -4.5
   - *B.   6.0
   - C.   18
   - D. -18

5. If $2x - 5 = 7x - 15$, what does x equal?
   - A.   4
   - *B.   2
   - C. -4
   - D. -2

6. In a basketball game, Jessica made 75 percent of her 12 free throw attempts. Leanne made 60 percent of her 10 free throw attempts. How many more free throws did Jessica make than Leanne?
   - A. 1
   - B. 2
   - *C. 3
   - D. 4

7. A park in the shape of a rectangle is 325 meters long and 100 meters wide. What is the measure of the perimeter of the park?

  *A. 850 meters
   B. 750 meters
   C. 525 meters
   D. 425 meters

Matching Items

	I		II
F	1. 3/4	A.	0.060
C	2. 3/5	B.	0.500
D	3. 5/8	C.	0.600
A	4. 3/50	D.	0.625
B	5. 13/26	E.	0.670
		F.	0.750
		G.	0.875

Sample test items were prepared by John Tarr, Malcolm Price Laboratory School, University of Northern Iowa, Cedar Falls.

MUSIC

True-False Items

__F__ 1. The most likely meter for the example above would be 2/4.

__T__ 2. A performer will adjust the written dynamic markings to fit various performance conditions.

__F__ 3. Accurate tuning of one's instrument to concert B-flat assures that all other notes will be played in tune.

__F__ 4. A key signature containing three flats indicates that the music to follow must be in the key of E-flat.

Multiple-Choice Items

1. Which music direction is *least* likely to appear in the famous march "The Thunderer" (Sousa)?
    - A. tacet 1X
    - B. simile
    - C. marcato
    - *D. con sordino

2. Which of the following sets shows tempo markings in a correct slow-to-fast order?
    - A. andante-adagio-vivace
    - B. allegro-andante-presto
    - *C. largo-moderato-allegro
    - D. andante-largo-presto

3. The preceding example appears to be scored for which combination of instruments (in score order)?

    A. trumpet-horn-trombone

  *B. violin-clarinet-cello

    C. flute-clarinet-string bass

    D. violin-viola-cello

Matching Items

You will hear five short excerpts (about 45 seconds each) of unfamiliar concert band pieces. Use the clues provided with each title in column I to match the pieces with the letters in column II.

I	II
___ 1. *Ecossaise* (Beethoven): homophonic texture, strong accents, repetition of short sections, detached style.	A. 1st excerpt
___ 2. "Siciliana" from *A Little Concert Suite* (Reed): compound meter, legato style, melody predominantly set in woodwinds, homophonic texture.	B. 2d excerpt
___ 3. *Lyric Essay* (Coakley): legato style, polyphonic texture, duple meter, brief baritone solo.	C. 3d excerpt
___ 4. "A Toye" from *Giles Farnaby Suite* (arr. Wiggins): alternating homophonic and polyphonic textures, duple meter, minor mode, mixture of detached and legato styles.	D. 4th excerpt
___ 5. *Scottish Rhapsody* (Grundman): colorful effects, use of folk song material, meter changes, unusual voicings.	E. 5th excerpt

Essay Item

Most successful pieces of music show a balance between contrast and repetition. Why? In "Etude No. 3," how does the composer create repetition and contrast?

Points for grading

Structure (15 points)

- Perception of organization in music seems necessary for enjoyment (5 points).
- Repetition and contrast are essential elements of musical organization and structure (3 points).
- Repetition and contrast may help define organization and structure at several levels (3 points).
- The elements of music used to create repetition and contrast may include rhythm, melody, harmony, tone color, text, and form (1 point for each element—4 points total).

Mixture of novel and known (10 points)

- Humans seem to find stimuli that are a mixture of novel and known information to be the most interesting (4 points).
- Too much novel information in a musical work is often perceived as chaotic (3 points); too much repetition of known information is perceived as boring, dry, or academic (3 points).

Sample test items were prepared by Mark Ellis, The Ohio State University at Mansfield.

PHYSICAL EDUCATION

True-False Items

 F 1. In shuffleboard, the first player to score 21 points wins.

 T 2. Each player in shuffleboard has four discs.

 T 3. It is possible to score 10 points off in shuffleboard.

 F 4. Shuffleboard must be played by four players.

 F 5. In shuffleboard, there are five different areas in which to score points.

Multiple-Choice Items

1. In golf, a score of three on a 125-yard hole is a/an
   *A. par.
   B. bogey.
   C. birdie.
   D. eagle.

2. The most common grip used by professional golfers is the
   A. overlapping.
   *B. interlocking.
   C. baseball.
   D. overlocking.

3. In golf, which is a two-stroke penalty?
   A. hitting into the woods
   B. teeing off out of order
   C. throwing a club
   *D. grounding a club in a hazard

4. In golf, an apron refers to the
   A. putting green.
   *B. grass located adjacent to the green.
   C. sand trap beside a green.
   D. towel used to wipe off dirty clubs.

5. Which club would a golfer use if the ball were 50 yards from the hole?
   A. driver
   B. brassie
   *C. wedge
   D. three iron

Matching Items

	I		II
F	1. love	A.	archery
D	2. eagle	B.	badminton
H	3. ringer	C.	shuffleboard
B	4. shuttlecock	D.	golf
C	5. disc	E.	bowling
G	6. paddle	F.	tennis
		G.	table tennis
		H.	horseshoes
		I.	baseball

Essay Item

Describe five gymnastic events and draw a picture of the apparatus used in each event. Identify a specific stunt that is performed on each apparatus.

Points for grading

- Five gymnastic events (10 points).
- Drawing of apparatus for five gymnastic events (10 points).
- Specific stunt for each event (10 points).

Sample test items were prepared by Thomas L. Tucker, Lakota Schools, Rising Sun, Ohio.

PHYSICS

True-False Items

__T__ 1. Fifty-six miles is a greater distance than 80 kilometers.

__T__ 2. The slope of a velocity-time curve (graph) defines acceleration.

__F__ 3. Constant speed and constant acceleration are the same motion.

__F__ 4. Mass is a vector quantity.

__F__ 5. Mass and weight are measured in the same units.

__F__ 6. The "order of magnitude" of the number 5.3×10^4 is four.

__F__ 7. The trigonometric function sine is equal to the adjacent side divided by the hypotenuse.

__T__ 8. The SI unit for velocity is meters/second.

__T__ 9. Sliding friction is less than static friction.

__T__ 10. It is possible for a vector of 5 units in length to be added to a vector of 6 units in length and end up with a vector of 8 units in length.

Multiple-Choice Items

1. In mechanics, which three fundamental units are used to measure quantities?
    A. length, mass, and speed
    B. mass, speed, and time
    *C. mass, length, and time
    D. length, speed, and time

2. A weight attached to a spring is vibrating up and down in simple harmonic motion. At which place is the weight undergoing minimum acceleration?
    A. top of the vibration
    *B. middle of the vibration
    C. bottom of the vibration
    D. same at all points

3. How do gravitational forces compare with electrical forces?
    *A. much smaller
    B. smaller
    C. larger
    D. much larger

4. In the impulse-momentum equation ft = mv, which variable is most important in the coach's request to "follow through"?
    A. force (f)
    *B. time (t)
    C. mass (m)
    D. velocity (v)

5. Which of the following is a scalar quantity?
    A. acceleration
    B. force
    C. velocity
    *D. work

6. The value of the gravitational constant G was measured about 1800 by
   A. Newton.
   B. Kepler.
   *C. Cavendish.
   D. Brahe.

7. Which of the following is a unit of energy?
   A. watt
   B. newton-second
   C. joule/second
   *D. joule

8. Waves provide a means of transferring
   A. matter.
   B. liquids.
   C. particles.
   *D. energy.

9. Sound waves cannot travel through
   A. water.
   B. air.
   *C. vacuum.
   D. steel.

Matching Items

I	II
__E__ 1. $Y = 5X$	A.
__B__ 2. $Y = 7X^2$	B.
__D__ 3. $Y = 4$	C.
__A__ 4. $Y = 3\sqrt{X}$	D.
__C__ 5. $XY = 6$	E.
	F.

84

Essay Items

A merry-go-round is 42 feet in diameter. It is making 5 complete revolutions in two minutes. A small child slips from a horse and falls off the edge. At what speed does the child hit the ground?

Points for Grading
- Correct procedure (5 points).
- Answer: 5.5 feet/second or 3.4 mph (5 points).

The famous cliff divers at Acapulco, Mexico, dive from a cliff 60 meters high. Rocks extend outward at the bottom of the cliff for about 20 meters. What is the minimum horizontal velocity the divers must have in order to clear the rocks below?

Points for Grading
- Correct procedure (5 points).
- Answer: 5.7 meters/second (5 points).

Sample test items were prepared by Oliver Eason, Cedar Falls High School, Iowa.

SCIENCE

True-False Items

T   1. The sun is the center of the solar system.

F   2. A light year measures time.

F   3. On a clear night, Polaris can be seen directly overhead.

F   4. The main fuel of a star is oxygen.

T   5. Jupiter is the largest planet in the solar system.

Multiple-Choice Items

1. The sun is a/an
    *A. middle-aged star.
    B. old star.
    C. young star.
    D. dead star.

2. A star's energy is produced by
    A. burning.
    *B. fusion.
    C. reflection.
    D. chemical reaction.

3. The moon revolves around the earth in
    A. 24 hours.
    B. 7 days.
    *C. 27 ⅓ days.
    D. 365 days.

4. Meteoroids that reach the earth's surface are
    A. asteroids.
    B. comets.
    C. meteors.
    *D. meteorites.

5. Planets are observed because they
    A. burn.
    B. give off their own light.
    *C. reflect the sun's light.
    D. reflect the earth's light.

Matching Items

	I		II
D	1. a telescope that uses no light	A.	parallax
B	2. uses a concave mirror	B.	reflecting telescope
A	3. a procedure for measuring star distance	C.	refracting telescope
C	4. uses a convex lens	D.	radio telescope
H	5. separates light into colors	E.	chemical reaction
		F.	reflecting microscope
		G.	chemical fusion
		H.	spectroscope

Essay Item

How do astronomers know if galaxies are moving closer to or away from the earth?

Points for grading

- Doppler effect (1 point).
- Blue-shift in spectrum—toward (1 point).
- Red-shift in spectrum—away (1 point).

Sample test items were prepared by William Simpson, Holmes Junior High School, Cedar Falls, Iowa.

SOCIAL STUDIES

True-False Items

__T__ 1. Geographers have accepted the theory of "Continental Drift" as an explanation of past and present configurations of continents.

__T__ 2. The climate of land next to large bodies of water will change less rapidly than the climate farther inland.

__F__ 3. Humid tropical climates are found within five degrees latitude north and south of the Tropics of Cancer and Capricorn.

Use the following graph to answer statements 4 and 5.

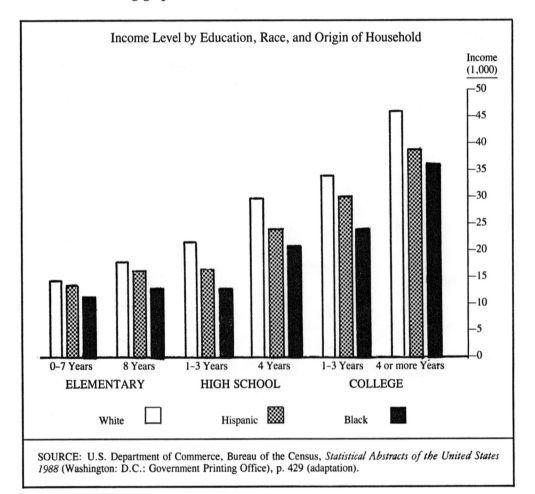

Income Level by Education, Race, and Origin of Household

SOURCE: U.S. Department of Commerce, Bureau of the Census, *Statistical Abstracts of the United States 1988* (Washington: D.C.: Government Printing Office), p. 429 (adaptation).

__F__ 4. Black, white, and Hispanic people with one to three years of college make over $35,000 a year.

__T__ 5. Black, white, and Hispanic people with eight years of schooling make less money than persons with four years of high school.

Multiple-Choice Items

1   Which of the following statements is fact rather than opinion?
    A. Federal aid to local communities increases the national debt.
    *B. Since the 1950s, the percentage of persons over age 65 has been increasing in the United States.
    C. America's involvement in the Vietnam War increased young people's distrust of government.
    D. Voting for Republicans is a vote to cut federal spending.

Read the following statement and respond to item 2.

Sue: I am so tired of reading about criminals who are freed by the courts because the police did not interrogate them properly. Courts should not free guilty people because of technicalities. Suspects should be required to answer all the questions the police ask when they are apprehended.

Bill: I am not so sure I agree with you. After all, those "technicalities" during interrogation are designed to prevent police from obtaining forced confessions from people. Without rules governing interrogation procedures, what is to prevent the police from just grabbing anybody and forcing the person to confess to a crime?

---

2. Sue and Bill's dialogue indicates that they have a value conflict over
    A. individual guilt versus legal technicalities.
    *B. police power versus protection of the innocent.
    C. court procedures versus public safety.
    D. individual rights versus the right of police.

Essay Item

Provide a solution to the current acid rain problem in northeastern United States and southeastern Canada. Explain why your solution is more effective than previously proposed approaches.

Points for grading
  • United States and Canadian government proposals are described (20 points).
  • Industry proposals are mentioned (10 points).
  • Student's proposal indicates a reasonable understanding of the problem with possible solution (20 points.)

Sample test items were prepared by Stephen Rose, Malcolm Price Laboratory School, University of Northern Iowa, Cedar Falls.

SPANISH

True-False Items

__T__ 1. <u>Ciento</u> is shortened to <u>cien</u> before all nouns and before <u>mil</u> and <u>millones</u>.

__F__ 2. <u>Un</u> is omitted before <u>ciento</u> but is used before <u>mil</u> and <u>millon</u>.

__T__ 3. The word <u>y</u> is used between tens and units in numbers.

__T__ 4. If the direct object of a verb is a noun that refers to a definite person, the word <u>a</u> is used in front of the direct object.

__F__ 5. When <u>salir</u> is followed by an object, Spanish uses the preposition <u>a</u> in front of the object.

__T__ 6. If the action in the dependent clause takes place in the past, the past subjunctive may be used in a dependent clause that follows a main clause verb of present, future, or present perfect tense.

__T__ 7. The future, the conditional, or the present subjunctive is not used after <u>si</u> meaning ''if.''

Multiple-Choice Items

1. If he is in his room, he's studying.
    A. Si estuviera en su cuarto, estudiaría.
    B. Si es en su cuarto, estudia.
  *C. Si está en su cuarto, estudia.
    D. Si hubiera estado en su cuarto, está estudiando.

2. If he were here, he would tell us.
  *A. Si estuviera aquí, nos diría.
    B. Si fuera aquí, nos daria.
    C. Si está aquí, nos dice.
    D. Si hubiera sido aqui, nos diría.

3. If he had traveled more, he would have obtained the job.
    A. Si viaja más, obtendrá el puesto.
  *B. Si hubiera viajado mas, habría obtenido el puesto.
    C. Si había viajado más, hubiera obtenido el puesto.
    D. Si viajara mas, habría obtenido el puesto.

4. If I were you, I wouldn't say that.
  *A. Si fuera usted, no diría eso.
    B. Si estuviera usted, no diría eso.
    C. Si está usted, no diría eso.
    D. Si fuera usted, no daría eso.

Matching Items

	I		II
I	1. patron saint of Mexico	A.	Taxco
F	2. Aztec capital city	B.	Guadalajara
A	3. famous silver mining city	C.	Chapultepec
C	4. palace and park in Mexico City	D.	Xochimilco
J	5. leader of the Mexican Revolution in 1810	E.	Teotihuacán
E	6. ancient ruins north of Mexico City	F.	Tenochtitlán
H	7. feathered serpent god	G.	Chichén Itzá
		H.	Quetzelcoatl
		I.	Guadalupe
		J.	Hidalgo

Essay Item

Write a dialogue in Spanish for the following situation:

You wish to rent a room in a hotel and tell the desk clerk you want a room with two beds. You want three bars of soap, two towels, and comfortable beds. The room should face the street and have a good view. You ask what time meals are served and tell the clerk you will stay for a week.

Points for grading
- Dialogue includes all items specified (8 points).
- Present tense verbs (1 point).
- Expression <u>dar a</u> (1 point).
- Use of indefinite subject or reflexive substitute for passive voice when asking about meals (1 point).
- Use of future tense when indicating length of stay (1 point).

Sample test items were prepared by Carol Underwood, Bettsville Local Schools, Ohio.

GLOSSARY OF TERMS

Affective objectives emphasize feelings, emotions, attitudes, and values.

In a *bimodal distribution* two scores tie for most frequent occurrence.

Cognitive objectives emphasize intellectual tasks.

Concurrent validity compares a teacher-made test with a similar assessment measure.

Construct validity identifies the psychological traits or underlying constructs of a test.

Content validity is the most common type of validation used by teachers to ascertain if the test provides an accurate assessment of the instructional objectives.

Equivalent forms is a method of establishing reliability by correlating scores from two different, but equivalent, forms of a test.

A *frequency distribution* is a tally of scores for a particular test arranged from highest to lowest.

Item difficulty indicates the proportion of students who responded correctly to a test item.

Item discrimination provides an index of how an item discriminates between high- and low-scoring students.

The *Kuder-Richardson Formula 21 (KR21)* is a method of establishing reliability that requires a single administration of a test and uses the mean and standard deviation of the test scores.

The *mean* is the arithmetic average of test scores.

The *median* is the middle test score in a list of scores from highest to lowest.

The *mode* is the most frequent test score (the score made by the largest number of students) in a frequency distribution.

Negative discrimination occurs when more low- than high-scoring students respond correctly to a test item.

A *negatively skewed* distribution occurs when the longer tail of the distribution extends toward the negative (left) end of the distribution.

No discrimination occurs when an equal number of high- and low-scoring students respond correctly to a test item.

A *normal curve* represents a normal or symmetrical distribution of scores.

An *objective* is a communication device that specifies the knowledge, skills, and attitudes expected of students at the end of an instructional unit.

A *percentile rank* indicates the percentage of students in a class who obtained raw scores below a given score.

Positive discrimination occurs when more high- than low-scoring students respond correctly to a test item.

A *positively skewed* distribution occurs when the longer tail of the distribution extends toward the positive (right) end of the distribution.

Predictive validity correlates test performance with a future outcome.

Psychomotor objectives emphasize skill development and require neuromuscular coordination.

The *range* is the difference between the highest and lowest scores on a test.

Rank indicates the position of a score in relation to other scores.

A *raw score* is the actual score that a student receives on a test.

Reliability provides an estimate of the consistency of test results; it is expressed as a correlation coefficient reported on a scale ranging from 0.00 to 1.00.

A *response profile* provides an index of the frequency of student responses to test alternatives.

A *skewed distribution* is an asymmetrical distribution with a majority of scores at one end of the distribution.

The *Spearman-Brown Formula* is a correction formula applied to the correlation coefficient, which establishes a reliability coefficient for the entire test.

Split-half is a method of establishing reliability by correlating the scores from two halves of the same test.

Standard deviation is a measure of dispersion that indicates how scores within a distribution deviate from the mean.

A *T-score* represents the number of standard deviations a raw score is from the mean in a distribution. Unlike z-scores, T-scores do not use decimals or negative numbers.

Test-retest is a method of establishing reliability by correlating scores from two administrations of the same test to the same group of students in a given time interval.

In a *trimodal distribution* three scores tie for most frequent occurrence.

Validity is the extent to which a test measures what it was intended to measure.

A *z-score* represents the number of standard deviations a raw score is from the mean in a distribution.

BIBLIOGRAPHY

Adkins, D. C. *Test Construction: Development and Interpretation of Achievement Tests.* 2d ed. Columbus, Ohio: Charles E. Merrill, 1974.

American Psychological Association. *Standards for Educational and Psychological Testing.* Washington, D.C.: American Psychological Association, 1986.

Archbald, D. A., and Newmann, F. M. *Beyond Standardized Testing: Assessing Authentic Academic Achievement in the Secondary School.* Reston, Va.: National Association of Secondary School Principals, 1988.

Ball, D. W. "Level of Teacher Objectives and Their Classroom Tests: Match or Mismatch." *Journal of Social Studies Research* 10, no. 2 (1986): 27–31.

Bergman, J. *Understanding Educational Measurement and Evaluation.* Boston: Houghton Mifflin, 1981.

Bloom, B. S.; Englehart, M. D.; Furst, E. J.; Hill, W. H.; and Krathwohl, D. R. *Taxonomy of Educational Objectives: Handbook I, Cognitive Domain.* New York: David McKay, 1956.

Brown, F. G. *Measuring Classroom Achievement.* New York: Holt, Rinehart and Winston, 1981.

Carlson, S. B. "Creative Testing Ideas." *Social Science Record* 24, no. 1 (1987): 6–7.

Carter, K. "Test-Wiseness for Teachers and Students." *Educational Measurement: Issues and Practice* 5, no. 4 (1986): 20–23.

Cashin, W. E. *Improving Essay Tests.* Idea Paper No. 17. Manhattan, Kan.: Center for Faculty Evaluation and Development, Division of Continuing Education, Kansas State University, 1987.

Clegg, V. L., and Cashin, W. E. *Improving Multiple-Choice Tests.* Idea Paper No. 16. Manhattan, Kan.: Center for Faculty Evaluation and Development, Division of Continuing Education, Kansas State University, 1986.

Coker, D. R.; Kolstad, R. K.; and Sosa, A. H. "Improving Essay Tests: Structuring the Items and Scoring Responses." *Clearing House* 61, no. 6 (1988): 253–55.

Denova, C. C. *Test Construction for Training Evaluation.* New York: Van Nostrand Reinhold, 1979.

Ebel, R. L., and Frisbie, D. A. *Essentials of Educational Measurement.* 4th ed. Englewood Cliffs, N.J.: Prentice-Hall, 1986.

Erickson, R. C., and Wentling, T. L. *Measuring Student Growth: Techniques and Procedures for Occupational Education.* Urbana, Ill.: Griffon Press, 1988.

Green, K. E., and Stager, S. F. "Differences in Teacher Test and Item Use with Subject, Grade Level Taught, and Measurement Coursework." *Teacher Education and Practice* 4, no. 1 (1987): 55–61.

Gronlund, N. E. *How to Construct Achievement Tests.* 4th ed. Englewood Cliffs, N.J.: Prentice-Hall, 1988.

_____. *Measurement and Evaluation in Teaching.* 5th ed. New York: Macmillan, 1985.

_____. *Stating Objectives for Classroom Instruction.* 3d ed. New York: Macmillan, 1985.

Gulliksen, H. *Creating Better Classroom Tests.* Princeton, N.J.: Educational Testing Service, 1985.

Ingram, C. F. *Fundamentals of Educational Assessment*. New York: Van Nostrand Reinhold, 1980.

Karras, R. "Realistic Approach to Thinking Skills: Reform Multiple-Choice Questions." *Social Science Record* 22, no. 2 (1985): 38–43.

Kelleghan, G. F.; Madaus, G. F., and Airasian, P. W. *The Effects of Standardized Testing*. Norwell, Mass.: Kluwer Academic, 1981.

Kirby, P. C., and Oescher, J. "Testing for Critical Thinking: Improving Test Development and Evaluation Skills of Classroom Teachers." Paper presented at the annual meeting of the Mid-South Educational Research Association, Mobile, Alabama, November 1987.

Kline, P. A. *Handbook of Test Construction: Introduction to Psychometric Design*. New York: Methuen, 1986.

Kolstad, R. K., and Briggs, L. P. "The Application of Item Analysis to Classroom Achievement Tests." *Education* 105, no. 1 (1984): 70–72.

Krathwohl, D. R., Bloom, B. S.; and Masia, B. B. *Taxonomy of Educational Objectives: Handbook II, Affective Domain*. New York: David McKay, 1964.

Kryspin, W. J., and Feldhusen, J. F. *Developing Classroom Tests: A Guide for Writing and Evaluating Test Items*. Minneapolis: Burgess, 1974.

Lang, R. M. *Strategies for Improving Teacher-Made Tests*. DeKalb, Ill.: Northern Illinois University, 1983. ERIC Document Reproduction Service. ED 247 261.

Leuba, R. J. "Machine-Scored Testing, Part 1: Purposes, Principles, and Practices." *Engineering Education* 77, no. 2 (1986): 89–95.

Linn, R. L. *Educational Measurement*. 3d ed. New York: Macmillan, 1989.

Lodish, E. "Test Writing Made Simple: Generate Tests and Worksheets Electronically." *Electronic Learning* 5, no. 5 (1986): 28, 30, 68.

Mager, R. F. *Preparing Instructional Objectives*. 2d ed. Belmont, Calif.: Pitman Management and Training, 1984.

Marso, R. N. "Testing Practices and Test Item Preferences of Classroom Teachers." Paper presented at the annual meeting of the Midwestern Educational Research Association, Chicago, October 1985.

Marso, R. N., and Pigge, F. L. "An Analysis of Teacher-Made Tests: Testing Practices, Cognitive Demands, and Item Construction Errors." Paper presented at the annual meeting of the National Council on Measurement in Education, New Orleans, April 1988.

McAuthur, D. L. *Alternative Approaches to the Assessment of Achievement*. Norwell, Mass.: Kluwer Academic, 1987.

Miller, P. W. "Review of LXR•TEST (Version 3.1) by Logic Extension Resources." *Journal of Industrial Teacher Education* 26, no. 2 (1989): 63–65.

———. "Developing Good Tests in Technical Education." *Journal of Vocational Education* 63, no. 5 (1988): 51–52.

———. "The Effects of Selected Industrial Arts Activities on Educable Mentally Retarded Students' Achievement and Retention of Metric Linear Concepts." Doctoral dissertation, The Ohio State University, 1977. *Dissertation Abstracts International* 38, 4627A. University Microfilms No. 7731934.

Miller, P. W., and Erickson, H. E. *Teacher-Written Student Tests: A Guide for Planning, Creating, Administering, and Assessing*. Washington, D.C.: National Education Association, 1985.

Miller, W. R. *Instructors and Their Jobs*. Homewood, Ill.: American Technical Publishers, 1990.

Nimmer, D. N. "Multiple True-False Classroom Tests." *Clearing House* 56, no. 6 (1983): 257–58.

_____. "Measures of Validity, Reliability, and Item Analysis for Classroom Tests." *Clearing House* 58, no. 3 (1984): 138–40.

Nitko, A. J. *Educational Tests and Measurements: An Introduction.* New York: Harcourt Brace Jovanovich, 1983.

O'Brien, N. P. *Test Construction: A Bibliography of Selected Resources.* New York: Greenwood Press, 1988.

Popham, J. W. *Modern Educational Measurement.* Englewood Cliffs, N.J.: Prentice-Hall, 1981.

Reneau, F. W. "Framing the A+ Test." *Journal of Vocational Education* 64, no. 5 (1989): 34–35.

Schoer, L. A. *Test Construction: A Programmed Guide.* Boston: Allyn and Bacon, 1970.

Simpson, E. J. "The Classification of Educational Objectives in the Psychomotor Domain." In *The Psychomotor Domain.* Vol. 3. Washington, D.C.: Gryphon House, 1972.

Smith, C. W. "100 Ways to Improve and Use Teacher-Made Tests." *Illinois Schools Journal* 66, no. 3 (1987): 20–26.

Steinmetz, J. E.; Romano, A. G.; and Patterson, M. M. "Statistical Programs for the Apple II Microcomputer." *Behavior Research Methods and Instrumentation* 13, no. 5 (1981): 702.

Stiggins, R. J., and Bridgeford, N. J. "The Ecology of Classroom Assessment." *Journal of Educational Measurement* 22, no. 4 (1985): 271–86.

Stiggins, R. J.; Conklin, N. F.; and Bridgeford, N. J. "Classroom Assessment: A Key to Effective Education." *Educational Measurement: Issues and Practice* 5, no. 2 (1986): 5–17.

Stiggins, R. J.; Rubel, E.; and Quellmalz, E. *Measuring Thinking Skills in the Classroom.* Washington, D.C.: National Education Association, 1988.

Stith, J. H., and Constantine, A. G. "Writing Better Physics Exams." *Physics Teacher* 26, no. 3 (1988): 138–44.

Swezey, R. W. *Individual Performance Assessment: An Approach to Criterion-Referenced Test Development.* Reston, Va.: Reston Publishing, 1981.

Thorndike, R., and Hagen, E. *Measurement and Evaluation in Psychology and Education.* New York: Macmillan, 1986.

Tchudi, S. N., and Yates, J. *Teaching Writing in the Content Areas: Senior High School.* Washington, D.C.: National Education Association, 1983.

Wilson, L. R.; Scherbeth, B. C.; Brickel, H. M.; Mayo, S. T.; and Paul, R. H. *Determining Validity and Reliability of Locally Developed Assessments—1988.* Springfield, Ill.: Illinois State Board of Education, 1988. ERIC Document Reproduction Service. ED 300 417.

Wolansky, W. D. "Evaluating Student Performance in Vocational Education." *Educational Horizons* 65, no. 1 (1988): 42–44.